R.A.W. Hitman 2

S. Hussain Zaidi is a veteran investigative, crime and terror reporter with a career spanning decades. His previous books include *Mafia Queens of Mumbai, Dongri to Dubai, Byculla to Bangkok, Mumbai Avengers* and *R.A.W. Hitman: The Real Story of Agent Lima*, some of which have been adapted into popular Bollywood films. Hussain Zaidi lives with his family in Mumbai.

Kashif Mashaikh's literary works span crime, thriller and dark fiction. His debut novel, *Mortuary Tales*, a modern-day retelling of Vikram-Betaal, was well received by the audiences. Kashif graduated with a degree in computer science from the University of Mumbai.

R.A.W. Hitman 2

The Assassinations

KASHIF MASHAIKH AND LUCKY BISHT

Created by

S. HUSSAIN ZAIDI

SIMON &
SCHUSTER

London · New York · Sydney · Toronto · New Delhi

First published in India by Simon & Schuster India, 2024

3 5 7 9 10 8 6 4 2

Simon & Schuster India
818, Indraprakash Building,
21, Barakhamba Road,
New Delhi 110001.

www.simonandschuster.co.in

Paperback ISBN: 978-81-979492-0-3
eBook ISBN: 978-81-979492-7-2

Simon & Schuster: Celebrating 100 Years of Publishing in 2024

Typeset in India by SÜRYA, New Delhi
Printed and bound in India by Replika Press Pvt. Ltd.

CONTENTS

Prologue

There has been no better chronicler-in-chief of the Mumbai mafia than S. Hussain Zaidi, former investigative journalist and the author of fourteen best-selling books. His thirst for stories have led him to far lands of foreign shores and dark corners of many cities to unearth gems which may have otherwise remained undiscovered. Starting from his debut book, *Black Friday: The True Story of the Bombay Bomb Blasts*, each of Mr Zaidi's projects have been meticulously researched.

It was during the research of one such book that he came across Laxman "Lucky" Bisht, a former National Security Guard (NSG) commando, who revealed that he was once made the prime accused in a sensational double murder case by the Uttarakhand Police in 2011. Lucky had spent a significant amount of time in jail before being acquitted in the case. He later met Mr Zaidi in Mumbai to narrate his tale which was tightly interwoven with that of a mysterious secret service operative named Agent Lima.

Lucky Bisht, a man marked by his military precision and stoic demeanour, recounted the events leading up to his arrest with a flavour that Mr Zaidi found both compelling and chilling. Lucky would endure a great ordeal from the moment the Uttarakhand

Police stormed into his house. He was arrested and subjected to gruelling interrogations, including the threat of a fake encounter by the cops.

The story of Lucky Bisht and Agent Lima was brought to life by Mr Zaidi in his best-selling book, *RAW Hitman: The Real Story of Agent Lima*.

As per Lucky, in September 2011, the brutal murders of gangsters Raju Pargai and Amit Arya shook the state of Uttarakhand. Raju Pargai was a notorious figure in the criminal underworld, deeply involved in activities such as murder, kidnapping and extortion. Pargai's operations included smuggling weapons into India, utilising routes through Nepal to facilitate this illegal arms trade.

Raju Pargai's foray into cross-border crime drew the attention of—the *Agency*. The organisation dispatched a covert operative named Agent Lima to eliminate Pargai. Agent Lima used a cover identity and befriended Pargai on the pretext of securing a profitable arms deal for him and his gang.

Trapped in Lima's plan, on the night of 5 September 2011, Pargai and Arya were driving through the forests of Uttarakhand, enroute to meet the *arms supplier* along with Agent Lima, who was sprawled in the backseat of the car. Lima asked Pargai to stop the car as he wanted to relieve himself. The car stopped near an area known as Shyamkhet. When Lima returned, he tapped on the window of the passenger side of the front seat which was rolled down by Arya.

Agent Lima then fired a single bullet which entered Arya's skull and exited from Pargai's temple. Both Pargai and Arya were found dead in the front seats of their car.

The following day, Laxman "Lucky" Bisht, an NSG commando, was arrested in Haldwani, accused of the murders. Lucky was tortured by the cops while the media turned him into a mafia boss.

He was labelled as "Commando Bhai" by the newspapers and was accused of running his own gang.

RAW Hitman: The Real Story of Agent Lima covered Lucky's training as a soldier in Israel, and his work as a security officer for top politicians, including Prime Minister Narendra Modi who was then the chief minister of Gujarat.

Lucky described Agent Lima with an almost shadowed tone, depicting a man who operated with stealth, his every move calculated, his identity a tightly guarded secret. The more Bisht revealed, the clearer it became that this was not just a simple case of mistaken identity but also a complex web of deceit and danger. The book also detailed Agent Lima's audacious plan to eliminate Pargai and Arya.

This sparked a mystery: why did Lucky spend over five years tangled in the case, transferred between jails and repeatedly denied bail, despite his government ties? And why were constant threats made to his life in jail?

Lucky Bisht fought a long-standing legal battle which ultimately led to his acquittal. His harrowing tale and Agent Lima's lethal professionalism captured the imagination of many. A conversation between Mr Zaidi and Lucky on the same subject racked up approximately two and a half million views on Mr Zaidi's official YouTube channel.

People wanted to know more about Agent Lima, and hear about his missions. A pact was formed between Mr Zaidi and Lucky. They would collaborate to unveil the clandestine operations and the thrilling missions of the enigma known as Agent Lima. A treasure trove of stories was unravelled between them.

And this is how it unfolded...

KASHIF MASHAIKH

one

Operation Monopoly

Mr Zaidi met Lucky Bisht at a restaurant near Mumbai's iconic Juhu Beach. Across its golden sands, the rhythmic waves of the Arabian Sea met the lively crowd of locals and tourists. Inside the hotel, the aroma of fresh seafood wafted through the air, mingling with the sea breeze, creating an atmosphere that was quintessentially Mumbai.

The restaurant exuded an old-world charm with its wooden interiors, vintage posters and soft, ambient lighting.

As the two men settled into their conversation, Mr Zaidi's mind shifted to the world of espionage. He began recounting the infamous case of Alexander Litvinenko, a former Federal Security Service (FSB, the principal security agency of Russia and the primary successor to the KGB or Committee for State Security) officer who had turned into a vocal critic of the Kremlin. Litvinenko's assassination in 2006 shocked the whole world and shed light on the deadly lengths to which secret service agencies could go.

"Litvinenko was living in London when he suddenly fell ill after meeting two former Russian agents at a hotel," Mr Zaidi said, his voice taking on a storyteller's cadence. "It was later discovered that he had been poisoned with polonium-210, a rare and highly radioactive substance."

Secret service agents had slipped the poison into his tea, leading to a slow and agonising death. His condition deteriorated rapidly. Within weeks, Litvinenko was in a critical state. Despite the best efforts of medical professionals, he passed away and left behind a trail of questions and suspicions. The incident had significant political repercussions, straining relations between Russia and the United Kingdom.

Lucky Bisht listened intently. The use of polonium-210 was particularly chilling due to its rarity and lethality. It was clear that only a state actor could have access to such a substance, pointing fingers squarely at the government.

"Agent Lima was also once involved in a mission to eliminate a target using a deadly poison," Lucky revealed, his voice low and steady.

Zaidi's eyes widened with intrigue. "Really? What happened?"

"There's much to tell," Lucky said. "And even more to uncover."

***

September 2020: Lal Mohammad sat in the sparsely lit Jammu Danda Police Station in Gokarneshwor, Nepal. His eyes flickered around the room as if he was surrounded by ghosts. He leaned forward, the chair creaking beneath, and cleared his throat. The police officer across from him, a man in his forties, had a thick moustache and tired eyes. The officer regarded him with a mix of suspicion. Lal Mohammad's eyes darted to the door as if he was expecting someone to burst in. The departmental voice of the police officer pulled him back to the moment.

"So you need police protection?" the officer asked. "Why?"

Lal Mohammad took a deep breath. "Some men have been following me," he said, his voice trembling. "They're watching my movements. They're out to kill me."

"Who are these men?" the officer asked. "Why do they want to kill you?"

"Eight years ago, they killed one of my associates." Lal Mohammad paused. "He died as if a curse had been placed upon him. Then the killers vanished without a trace." Another pause. "Now they've returned. And they're after me."

"Why did they kill your associate?"

Lal Mohammad swallowed his own spit. "I don't know."

But the truth was that he knew *bloody well* why those men killed his associate and why they wanted to kill him. Lal Mohammad, a permanent resident of Goudita Municipality-10 Manharwa in Sarlahi, had a complex past. Initially, he had been a contract killer. For six years, he managed a garment business in Kathmandu. But his life took a dark turn on the evening of 4 July 2007, when a man named Balram Patuwa of Bara was shot dead at Anamnagar Dhobi Khola. Out of the five accused, Lal Mohammad was swiftly apprehended by the police.

After nearly ten years in prison, he was released on 24 July 2017 through a government amnesty. Freed from the confines of his cell, Lal Mohammad resumed his garment business under the name Avenger Enterprises.

The Indian Intelligence Agency, Research and Analysis Wing (RAW), reported that Lal Mohammad played a pivotal role as a middleman in counterfeit currency transactions in Nepal. During this period, he was implicated in the murder plot of Iltaf Hussain Ansari and maintained associations with the infamous Dawood Ibrahim and the Inter-Services Intelligence (ISI).

Dawood Ibrahim, the infamous underworld don from Mumbai, had extended his nefarious reach into various criminal enterprises.

Among his many illicit ventures with the ISI, his involvement in the Indian fake currency racket was particularly insidious and targeted the very economic foundation of India.

The ISI's operation was not just a criminal act but a strategic attempt to undermine the Indian economy. Counterfeit currency, often indistinguishable from the genuine notes, flowed into India through various channels, including Nepal, Bangladesh and the Middle East.

The ISI's network was meticulously organised. Skilled engravers. High-quality printing presses. Strong distribution networks. Fake notes would be produced in secure locations, often within Pakistan and then smuggled into India via land, sea and air routes. These notes were then distributed through hawala transactions, local networks and even legitimate businesses, making their way into the Indian economy.

The counterfeit currency racket had multiple objectives. Financially, it aimed to destabilise the Indian economy by injecting large volumes of fake notes, causing inflation and devaluation of the rupee. Politically, it was a tool of asymmetric warfare, aiming to create economic uncertainty and strain on law enforcement agencies. It also facilitated criminal activities such as drug trafficking, human trafficking and terrorism.

Lal Mohammad's involvement in this racket was a significant cog in the larger machinery. Acting as a middleman, he facilitated the flow of counterfeit notes into Nepal and India, helping spread Dawood's influence across borders. But he didn't reveal all of this to the police officer at the Jammu Danda Police Station, of course.

The officer sighed, rubbing his temples. "So you're saying these men killed your associate in 2012. And have now come back to kill you for no reason?"

"Yes," Lal Mohammad whispered. "They're *dangerous*."

"All right, we'll see what we can do."

Lal Mohammad exhaled. He wasn't convinced. As he left the police station, the air felt heavy with his fears. Shadows seemed to stretch and twist, forming dark shapes that mirrored his anxiety. Lal Mohammad knew he was running out of time. The memories of his associate's death haunted him, the image of the man's lifeless body carved into his mind. He walked quickly, casting nervous glances over his shoulder. The streets of Kathmandu felt unfamiliar and threatening. He needed to find a way to disappear, to escape the invisible net closing in around him. The police protection was probably a Band-Aid on a tumour. He knew deep down that it wouldn't be enough. The men watching him were professionals, relentless in their pursuit of assassination. Just like they'd been in 2012.

***

2012: Agent Lima walked through the corridors of the Agency's office in New Delhi. The air was thick with the scent of aged paper and the muffled sounds of urgent conversations. He approached Colonel Sobhraj's office, a veteran of the Indian security apparatus. Sobhraj had led his men through the icy heights of Kargil and the insurgent-ridden jungles of the Northeast. His transition to the Agency was seamless; his strategic mind and battlefield acumen made him an invaluable asset. The Agency played a pivotal role in counter-terrorism, identifying and thwarting terrorist activities originating from abroad. It conducted covert operations, safeguarded India's strategic assets and provided intelligence support to the Indian Armed Forces. Additionally, it engaged in counter-intelligence to prevent infiltration by foreign agencies.

Over the years, Colonel Sobhraj had orchestrated numerous covert operations for the Agency, each more complex than the last. In 2006, he had led a covert unit tasked with infiltrating terrorist networks. His ability to blend into hostile environments and extract crucial intelligence without raising suspicion earned him the moniker: "The Phantom".

Lima, on the other hand, was a trained NSG commando who had also been deputed to the Agency.

The NSG was established in 1984 following the assassination of then Prime Minister Indira Gandhi. The unfortunate event had underscored the need for a specialised force to combat terrorism and protect high-risk VVIPs in India. Modelled after Germany's GSG 9 and Israel's Mossad and Sayeret Matkal, the NSG was conceived as a federal contingency deployment force to address serious internal security threats, including counter-terrorism, hijacking and hostage rescue operations.

As Lima entered the room, he found Sobhraj pacing, his stern face etched with the lines of countless missions.

"Agent Lima," Colonel Sobhraj said. His voice, deep and gravelly, commanded attention. "Take a seat."

Lima sat, his posture straight.

"We have a new mission," Sobhraj said. "Dismantle the fake currency network running across the northern side of our border." He paused. "This is deeply entrenched in an ISI-backed operation, flooding our economy with fake notes." Another pause. "Economic warfare."

The ISI was Pakistan's premier intelligence agency, established in 1948 to coordinate military intelligence across the country's armed forces. Over the decades, the ISI evolved into a powerful entity which wielded significant influence both within Pakistan and in the broader geopolitical arena.

Lima was well aware that the ISI was pushing 100 crores of fake currency every month into India from Nepal. By 2010, it was claimed that nearly 10,000 crores of fake currency was in circulation in India. The counterfeit notes were often of such high quality that they seamlessly entered the financial system, causing significant economic damage. Reports indicated that nearly 30 per cent of the fake currency seized in India originated from ISI-backed operations. Additionally, intelligence estimates suggested that the circulation of fake notes had contributed to a 20 per cent increase in black market transactions, further destabilising the Indian economy.

Animosity between the ISI and Indian intelligence agencies, particularly the RAW, dated back to the partition of British India in 1947, which led to the creation of India and Pakistan. Historical and territorial disputes, especially over Kashmir, fuelled a persistent state of conflict.

Colonel Sobhraj pulled a thick file from his desk and slid it across. Lima opened it, skimming through the detailed reports, photographs and intelligence briefs. Each page revealed the complexity of the operation, the layers of deception and danger.

"Your mission," Sobhraj said, "is to cut off the head of the snake. The fake currency network has to be dismantled."

Lima looked up, meeting Sobhraj's intense gaze. The mission was codenamed "Operation Monopoly"—a nod to the board game where fake currency is used to simulate economic dominance. This operation, however, dealt with real-world stakes, aiming to dismantle a network that was flooding the market with counterfeit money.

"Your first task is in Almora Jail," Sobhraj said. "There's a man inside, detailed in the file. He was caught with a significant amount of fake currency. Small fish with connections. Gain his trust. He will lead us to the bigger players."

Agent Lima had operated under several difficult settings, but this was the first time he was going to be lodged inside a prison. Almora Jail was established in 1872. Freedom fighters of the pre-Independence era like Mahatma Gandhi, Pt Jawahar Lal Nehru and Pt Govind Ballabh Pant had once been imprisoned in this facility by the Britishers. A lot of water had flown under the bridge since the country had gained independence, though. Enemies of the State had also changed. Elimination of enemies, however, was still a policy the Agency pursued with utmost seriousness.

Lima absorbed all the information, understanding the intricacies and the dangers. Almora Jail was filled with hardened criminals. Infiltrating it would be no small feat.

Sobhraj walked over to the window, staring out at the sprawling cityscape of Delhi.

"Every fake note in circulation is an attack on our economy," he said. "This *has* to stop."

Lima stood up; the file clutched in his hand. Colonel Sobhraj extended his hand, a rare and significant gesture. Lima grasped it firmly, feeling the weight of the promise they silently exchanged. As Lima left the office, the enormity of the task ahead settled over him. The fight against Lal Mohammad and the ISI had begun. And Agent Lima was at the forefront of this covert war.

***

Two havaldars flanked Agent Lima and led him towards barrack number 12 in Almora Jail; their footsteps echoing in the corridors. Almora Jail, officially known as Almora District Jail, was located in Uttarakhand. One of the oldest jails in the region, it was surrounded by dense forests and mountainous terrain. This added to the isolation of the facility.

Agent Lima had deeply ingrained the file containing the details of Operation Monopoly. From 2009 to 2012, the National Crime Records Bureau (NCRB) had reported the seizure of over 1.7 million fake Indian currency notes (FICN), valued at nearly INR 78 crore. Various Indian agencies, including the Reserve

Bank of India (RBI), Central Bureau of Investigation (CBI) and National Investigation Agency (NIA) were working collaboratively to combat the circulation of FICN. The NIA's Terror Funding and Fake Currency Cell (TFFC), established in 2010, also played a crucial role in these efforts.

Lima's entry in Almora Jail was a part of this larger game plan to take down an enemy of the nation. The man whom Lima was supposed to befriend was named Deepak Gupta. He was arrested with a sizable amount of fake currency, the roots of which could be traced to Kathmandu and Islamabad. The constables led Lima to a cell and opened the gate.

"Get inside," one of them said.

Lima entered the cell. The havaldars turned around and marched along the corridor until their footsteps were no longer audible. Agent Lima found the inmates of the cell huddled up in one corner, staring at him. He strutted in their direction and screwed his face into a menace.

"Which one of you *motherfuckers* knows where Deepak Gupta is?" Lima barked.

Nobody answered. They looked at each other with eyes wide open. Lima's swagger, and dominating voice had created quite an impression on the inmates. Silence prevailed. Finally, a boy standing in the back managed to squeal: *barrack number 15.* Lima craned his neck to spot the source of the voice. He crooked a finger and ordered the boy to step forward. The inmates parted, creating a path to allow the boy to pass. The boy scampered and told Lima everything that he knew about Gupta's activities in the jail—what time he woke up, what time he went for his walks and who were his friends or enemies inside Almora Jail.

Deepak Gupta was a history sheeter who was picked up by the UP Police from Ranikhet. He was involved in dealing with fake currency and was considered an important link in the ISI's operation of flooding the Indian market with duplicate currency. His bail application was due for a hearing soon, leaving little time for Lima to act.

Agent Lima, on the other hand, was lodged in barrack number 12 which was mainly occupied by those charged with minor offences. It took Lima three to four days to understand the dynamics of the jail and gel with the other inmates. He had also observed that a few of the inmates were obsessed with playing cricket in the grounds of the jail and Gupta was one of them. Lima started going to these games.

One day, he joined a match in progress. He grabbed a bat, feeling the willow under his hands. He waited for the bowler to take his run-up. When the ball came his way, he swung hard, sending it flying across the yard. Square cut. Cheers erupted from the spectators.

Deepak Gupta, a stocky man with a hawk-like gaze, stepped up next. Lima noticed the respect others showed him. Gupta's first few hits were solid.

"Good shot," Lima said, drawing Gupta's eyes.

During the breaks, Lima sat with the group, sharing the coarse jail chapatis and lentils. He made small talk, listening more than speaking. Gupta was intrigued by the new inmate's skills and demeanour and began to warm up to him. One afternoon, after an intense game, Lima and Gupta sat on the cracked stone steps of the yard. The sky above them was streaked with the last hues of sunset. Gupta handed Lima a bidi. Lima took a drag. Smoke curled in the still air.

"Where did you learn to play like that?" Gupta said.

Lima shrugged. "Here and there."

Days turned into weeks. With each game, their bond grew stronger. Lima learned about Gupta's routines, his habits and his influence within the jail. Gupta, in turn, grew to trust Lima, sharing snippets of his life. As their friendship developed, Lima began probing him on the crimes for which he was jailed. Gupta tried to pass himself off as an innocent civilian who was found in the wrong place at the wrong time.

"But the cops say that you were found with seventy thousand worth of fake currency," Lima said.

"Those bills were handed to me by someone with the intention to ensnare me," Gupta said. "I had no idea that the bills were fake."

Lima faked disappointment in his voice. "So all those rumours circulating in the jail about your contacts with fake currency racketeers are untrue?!" He paused. "I thought you were a big shot."

The remark left Gupta smouldering; a smarting slap on his bulging ego that he wouldn't be able to tolerate for long. Lima had hit the nail on its head with his psychological acumen. Gupta sulked for the next couple of days. Lima played cricket and spent time with him without making any mention of the subject of fake currency. On the third day, after the game of cricket, Gupta led Lima to a corner.

"Why were you so interested in fake currency?" Gupta said.

"Let's just say…I need those bills," Lima said.

"How much do you need?"

"Five lakh rupees of fake notes."

Gupta made some mental calculations. "Okay. The deal will take place in Nepal." He paused. "It will cost you two and a half lakhs. My commission is 10 per cent."

"What are the odds of the fake bills being spotted in the market?"

"My fake currency matches 99 per cent of the security features of the original. Micro-lettering. Intaglio. All of it."

Intaglio were raised prints that could be tactilely sensed by touch. This print was used by the RBI for the depiction of Mahatma Gandhi's portrait, the Reserve Bank seal, the guarantee and promise clause and the Ashoka Pillar Emblem on the left, along with the RBI governor's signature on denominations of several notes, including the five hundred and thousand rupee denominations.

"But still there is one per cent risk involved," Lima said.

"Stop being a nitpicker, you sick bastard," Gupta said. "Send your men and try the currency for yourself." He paused. "I'll connect your men to Parveen."

"Okay," Lima said. "Done."

They shook hands and Gupta returned to his barrack in the dark of the night which shrouded not only his movements but also the enormity of the deal he had just made with the inmate of barrack number 12.

***

Hours passed. Precincts of the Almora Jail were slowly getting enveloped in darkness. Lima moved through the corridors of the rundown prison. The moon hung low in the ink-black sky, casting a glow over the prison yard. Lima's cautious steps created no sound as they hit the floor. Years of covert training had honed his skills to perfection. He reached a corner where the faint glow of a flickering bulb barely lit the space. His heart raced as he fished out a contraband mobile phone he had smuggled inside.

He placed a call to Colonel Sobhraj and outlined the information he had extracted from Gupta, emphasising the imminent deal with the Nepali dealer, Parveen. Colonel Sobhraj listened intently, processing every detail.

"Move quickly," the Colonel said. "I will dispatch Chad and Zoro for the deal. Do you have anything else to say?"

"Gupta's asking for an extra fifty thousand. His commission."

"I'll get it approved." Colonel Sobhraj's voice crackled through the line. "Chad and Zoro will be in Nepal soon."

The call ended. Lima slipped the phone back into his hidden pocket. He retraced his steps with cautious movements until he reached his cell. At night, surrounded by the discordant snores of his fellow inmates, Lima lay on the stone-cold floor. He surveyed the confines of his cell. Tension in his muscles eased as his mind drifted, and in that fragile moment of calm, he felt weightless. He closed his eyes. He slept.

In Delhi, Lima's associates, Chad and Zoro, were getting ready to leave for Nepal.

Chad, formerly with the Indian Army, had developed a knack for logistics and strategic planning. His meticulous nature ensured that operations ran smoothly and efficiently. He was of medium build, with close-cropped hair and a perpetually serious expression. Zoro, formerly with the Delhi Police, was an expert in surveillance. His street smarts and ability to blend into any environment made him invaluable in undercover assignments. Tall and lean, with sharp features and penetrating eyes, Zoro had an air of quiet confidence. Together, they formed a skilled partnership. Both men were ready to play their part in Operation Monopoly.

Chad and Zoro's first stop was Mahendranagar in Nepal. The ninth largest city in Nepal, it's located five kilometres away from the east of the Indian border. Home to famous temples, a well-known pedestrian bridge and gorgeous lakes, it's a prominent tourist spot.

The duo reached the town and checked into a modest hotel. The building stood on a narrow street. Its faded sign was barely legible under layers of dust and grime. The room was small and sparsely furnished. A single window overlooked the chaotic street below. The bed creaked. The mattress sagged. The walls, once white, were now a patchwork of peeling paint and water stains.

Despite the room's shabby state, it offered refuge from the

prying eyes of the town. Chad and Zoro attuned their senses to the mission ahead. Soon enough, a group of Nepali men knocked on their door. The two knew instantly that it was Parveen, the point man of Deepak Gupta.

Parveen, a wiry man with sharp features and a perpetual look of unease, stepped into the room. His eyes darted around nervously. Dressed in a simple shirt and trousers, he carried a worn out duffle bag slung over his shoulder. His hands trembled slightly as he clutched the bag's strap tighter. Beads of sweat formed on his forehead.

"Where are the fakes?" Zoro asked.

"Here," Parveen said as he took the duffle bag off his shoulder.

Chad and Zoro absorbed his words. They nodded at Parveen, noticing his trembling hands and shifty eyes. Extensive years of dealings had only made him more paranoid about the business.

"You've got the cash, right?" Parveen said.

Chad pointed his eyes towards a briefcase in the corner of the room.

"I have four lakhs worth of fakes right now," Parveen said.

"*Baat paanch lakh ki hui thi* (the deal was worth five lakhs)," Chad retorted.

"Make the payment now," Parveen said. "The remaining one lakh will be delivered in three days."

"Sorry, my friend." Zoro shook his head. "We pay only for what we get."

Parveen could see that Zoro was unruffled even in an unknown territory. The exchange was made. And after much back and forth, which extended their stay in Nepal, Zoro and Chad received the remaining one lakh in fake currency and duly paid for it. The two operatives sneaked out of Nepal and returned to Delhi.

Lima received the news from the Agency that Gupta had delivered on his promise and that the fake currency had been delivered. The next step was to check the believability of the fake bills.

Lima once more snuck out of his cell to reach the deserted corner to make another clandestine call. He pulled out the phone and started pressing the number keys. This time it was Virender Chauhan, a trusted ally from Uttarakhand, that he wanted to speak with. Though Chauhan was a resourceful man who had helped Lima on several occasions, he was addicted to gambling.

"Chauhan," Lima said. "I've got a surprise for you."

"Which corner of the country are you in?"

"In our backyard, Almora. I have five lakh rupees to spare. Unfortunately, I can't enjoy this money. So I am looking for a benefactor."

"Why? Have you given up drinking?" Chauhan said and laughed. "What happened to you, man?"

Lima rolled his eyes. "Just take it, man. A gift from your friend."

"What do I do with that money?"

"Blow it on your choice of poison," Lima said. "Gamble it on a game of cards. And if you win, give me a share."

There was complete silence from Chauhan. Lima stifled a laugh. He knew that Chauhan's overflowing excitement had caused a block in his throat. A few seconds passed before Chauhan spoke again.

"Thanks, my man! You're a true friend," he said.

Lima could feel his friend's gratitude overflowing from the phone. But he burst into splits as soon as he had ended the call. Then he arranged for Chad and Zoro to deliver the bills to Chauhan.

Chauhan loved playing rummy at a gambling den and used Lima's gift to have the time of his life. Whatever remained from his losses in the betting ring, he spent on booze and other vices.

A few days later, Lima called him again. Chauhan told him that he had lost all the money.

"Don't feel bad buddy," Lima said. "The losses don't count for much."

"Why are you saying that?" Chauhan asked. "Have you hit a jackpot?"

"Same same but different," Lima said. "The bills were fake," Lima said. "I wanted to check if they'd work in the market."

"Rascal!" Chauhan said. "What if someone would have caught me?"

Lima laughed and hung up the phone. The next day, Lima met Gupta and informed him of the confirmation of the utility of the fake currency. Lima also delivered Gupta's commission to a place of his choice. Gupta's joy knew no bounds. He was elated and pulled Lima in an embrace.

"For our new alliance," Gupta said. "We should do more business while we share this space."

"Absolutely," Lima said. "But the men I sent are having a hard time trusting the finicky Parveen. And I want to place a bigger order this time."

"Not a problem. Let's meet in your barrack tonight."

Lima was slowly climbing up this ladder of the fake currency racket. He had enough exposure to this world and its people to know that a person such as Gupta would never hand him the main contact with whom he made regular dealings unless he had sufficient trust in the genuineness of the party or person he was dealing with. Late at night, Gupta ventured out of his cell and paid a visit to barrack number 12.

"Tell your men that they no longer have to deal with Parveen," he told Lima.

"Who will they be dealing with this time?"

"Hakeem," Gupta said, gesturing at the piece of paper. "He is

Parveen's boss. He's been managing my orders for a while now. There is someone who sits above him as well in the scheme of things. I am not sure."

Lima shook hands with Gupta. He knew that the "someone" above Hakeem was probably a reference to Lal Mohammad. But more leg work was required to reach the main man. For now, Lima decided that he would work with Hakeem and wait for the route leading to Lal Mohammad to be opened. The mission was crossing a crucial stage. And when the right time would come, Lima was ready to play his cards.

***

Lima couldn't say if Gupta was really ignorant about Lal Mohammad being the ringmaster of the entire racket or was simply feigning ignorance. But he simply tossed that concern aside for now as he had got Hakeem's contact information from Gupta. Hakeem's number was now resting safely inside his pocket. This was a significant key in the unravelling of the whole web of deception weaved by Lal Mohammad under the command of ISI.

There was no doubt as far as the Agency was concerned that Lal Mohammad was an agent hired by the ISI and D-company to accomplish their anti-Indian activities via Nepal.

Hakeem, on the other hand, was a heavily built man who always dressed up primly. He wore no other colour except white. For the next deal, Chad and Zoro met Hakeem in an upscale hotel in Nepal. The waiters would refill his drinks without him even needing to raise his fingers to call for their attention.

Hakeem leaned back, extracting a pristine cigar from his pocket. With a practised hand, he clipped the end and brought it to his lips. He struck a match, its flame dancing in the dim light, and carefully lit the cigar. He savoured the first draw, letting the rich smoke curl around him, a symbol of his control and power.

"Gupta is a *chutiya* of the highest order," Hakeem said. "He's been languishing in jail for a while."

"He speaks very highly of you," Chad said.

"Is it?" Hakeem said. "He must be a good man then." He laughed. "Gupta also told me that you guys have a big order. And it better be *big* because I hate people who waste my time." Hakeem smirked slightly. Chad and Zoro understood that Hakeem was trying to work on them. They were two seasoned operatives who knew that it was a tactic employed to invoke a feeling of shame in the opposite party to coax them into raising the amount.

Hakeem leaned forward and pressed his palms on the table. "So? How much?"

"*Fifty lakhs,*" Chad said.

Hakeem was impressed even if he did not want to show it. It was a deal worth twenty-five lakh Indian rupees. He nodded, and told them that he would arrange the money and call them again. This mission was costing the Agency a lot of money but the long-term benefits of ending this menace far outweighed the costs. Chad and Zoro left the meeting and returned to their hotel room. Now they'd have to wait for Hakeem to contact them again.

Meanwhile, back in India, Colonel Sobhraj was working behind the scenes to get Agent Lima out of jail. Also, he wanted to make sure that Deepak Gupta didn't get bail because the man could turn into a threat to the entire operation against Lal Mohammad. Outside the confines of Almora Jail, Gupta would want to get more involved in the currency transactions which were taking place between Sobhraj's agents and Lal Mohammad's men. And if Gupta sniffed a rat, the entire operation would collapse.

Sobhraj was successful in both his objectives. Gupta's bail was stalled. And Agent Lima was ready to walk out of Almora Jail and primed to join the mission with Chad and Zoro.

The Agency's operatives in Nepal started tracking Hakeem's phone number in the anticipation that he would contact Lal Mohammad for their new business deal worth twenty-five lakh rupees. The original plan was to back out of this deal once they would get Lal Mohammad's coordinates. But Hakeem was proving to be a hard operator. He didn't make any contact with his boss. On the contrary, he called up Chad and Zoro to inform them that the fakes were ready and they could make the payment and collect their *maal*. Chad and Zoro stalled him for a few days with different excuses while the two were still lodged in Nepal.

"We didn't carry over the full payment as it was risky," Chad said one time when Hakeem had called. "But our boss is getting it here in a few days."

"Who is your boss?"

"You'll meet him soon," Chad said.

Meanwhile, inside Almora Jail, Gupta pulled out his handkerchief from his pocket and wiped his sweaty face. He was stuffing the handkerchief back in his pocket when a hand came down on his shoulder from behind. He turned around. It was Lima.

"The men I sent to Hakeem do not seem much impressed," Lima said. "He is uncompromising and doesn't understand the difficulties involved in transferring the money."

"Maybe he is," Gupta said nonchalantly. "But you'll have to deal with him. There's no other way."

"I have bigger orders piling up. There has to be a better way of doing business."

Gupta shrugged. "Hakeem is as high as I go."

Gupta did not wait for Lima's response before starting to head off for his barracks. Lima had to think of a way to get him back to the discussion table. He doused his throat with a drink of indifference.

"Won't you be interested in knowing about the impending status of your bail?" Lima shouted.

Gupta stopped dead in his tracks. He turned and hurried back towards Lima. His tired demeanour had suddenly taken a stiff form. Now, he was all ears for what Lima had to say. Lima's words had pierced through Gupta's fatigue like a sharp blade. The fate of his freedom sparked a desperate intensity in his eyes.

"What do you know about my bail application?" Gupta said.

"You are a businessman, Gupta, and a seasoned one at that," Lima said. "Business is give and take."

"What will you *take* to give me the information I need?"

"Someone higher than Hakeem," Lima said. "I have a big deal coming up."

Gupta fell silent for a moment. His gaze wandered in the distance, beyond Lima, in an effort to comply with Lima's counsel and exert a little more pressure on his mind. Then, as if struck with a realisation, he remembered something.

"Once, I heard Hakeem talking to someone on his mobile phone," Gupta said. "The person on the other end was far superior to him. Besides, there was a large sum of money involved."

"How much?" Lima asked.

"Crores, perhaps."

"How can you be sure?"

"Am I jailed because I snatched a lollipop from a small kid, huh?" Gupta said. "I brush shoulders with people like Hakeem every day."

Lima gave a nod of affirmation.

"I gave you what I had," Gupta said. "Keep your end of the bargain."

Lima leaned over Gupta's shoulder. "A plan is being hatched on a high level to stop your bail application from being accepted."

"The cops can't stop my bail."

"My job was to inform you. Acting on my information is your choice. Or not."

"Who's sabotaging my bail?"

"The great entity who screws people like...*us*," Lima said. "Bharat sarkar."

Gupta was flustered. He promised to work it out with his lawyer and headed off to his cell. An impish smile played on Lima's lips. He knew that Gupta was helpless. The Agency's plan was well in place. There was little room for Gupta to manoeuvre.

Gupta's submissions had made Lima realise that Hakeem would only contact someone who was sitting over him when the deal was in crores. Meanwhile, the Agency's phone surveillance unit waited in vain for Hakeem to make a call to Lal Mohammad. Chad and Zoro kept stalling the deal for a week until Hakeem called them and threatened to cancel the deal if they didn't pay the money quick enough.

"When is your boss arriving with the money?!" Hakeem thundered.

"Two days, bhai," Chad replied. "Just two more days."

Somehow, Chad managed to keep Hakeem in control. But with this development, Colonel Sobhraj speeded Lima's release from the jail by collaborating with the Uttarakhand Police. As soon as Lima got the bail orders, he confided to Gupta that he was going to Nepal and meet Hakeem to conclude the current deal. He would also lay the groundwork for the next deal which would be worth in crores.

"And of course," Lima said, "you'll get your 10 per cent."

Lima promised that once he'd get out, he would move heaven and earth to arrange bail for Gupta. Those words were music to Gupta's ears. A few days later, Gupta's bail plea came up for hearing. The Agency had already made an arrangement with the judge who refused to grant bail to Gupta. It was then that Lima's reputation grew even stronger in Gupta's eyes, which were oblivious to what was happening behind the scenes.

***

Days later, Agent Lima landed in Nepal with the money. Chad and Zoro were relieved that Lima had arrived. A date was fixed with Hakeem to conclude a transaction which had been stalled for days. The trio got into a car and headed for the factory where Hakeem had invited them.

The Tata Sumo rattled along the bumpy dirt road, clattering in the wind that lashed through the open windows. The air conditioning wasn't working. Agent Lima's shirt got plastered to his back with sweat. His fingers gripped the steering wheel. Beside him, Chad chewed mint flavoured gum. Zoro scanned the desolate landscape from the back, his sole feeling the knife which was taped to his foot.

The factory loomed ahead; a hulking carcass against the twilight sky. Jagged teeth of broken windows grinned from the wooden frames. Lima pulled the vehicle to a stop beneath a rusted gantry. Silence stretched before a figure emerged from the factory's maw. Hakeem; a Nepali kukri glinted on his hip.

"Welcome, my friends." Hakeem's voice was a dry rustle in the wind. "Welcome!"

He led them through the darkened halls. Each creak of a floorboard sent a jolt through Lima's nerves. Finally, they reached a cavernous room which was lit by a single bare bulb. On a long iron table lay a duffel bag which was bulging like a pregnant yak. It contained fifty lakh FICN.

Hakeem's men, with their broad shoulders, flanked Lima. Chad's leg twitched. But Lima met his gaze, a silent order to hold. Hakeem unzipped the bag, the stench of plastic wafting out, acrid and suspicious. Lima's eyes spotted the telltale gleam of fresh ink. The edges of the bills were sharp—yet to be marred by the wear and tear of circulation.

Lima scrutinised a note carefully. The faint glimmer of a silver bromide thread caught his eye. Each note bore three distinct watermarks. Holding the note horizontally, Lima observed the digits "500" superimposed on the right side. It was a piece of work, as good as the original.

Hakeem's smile stretched wider. "See, gentlemen?" he said. "Trust is everything in this business."

Hakeem moved his hand towards the small of his back. *Was he going for his weapon?* Lima's heart hammered. They were inside the viper's nest. The only way out was a razor's edge underneath Zoro's foot. This was a game where the prize was a victory in waiting—or a one-way ticket to the Himalayas' icy embrace. But Hakeem only wanted to scratch an itch on his hips.

"Motherfucker hasn't bathed in ages," Lima whispered to Chad in a pahadi dialect.

The duo sniggered. Hakeem wanted to react, wanting in on the joke but Lima moved swiftly to push the bag with real Indian currency into Hakeem's direction. Twenty-five lakh rupees from the national exchequer. Gone; even if towards a larger cause.

Hakeem leaned back in his chair, extracting a cigar from his jacket pocket. Lima watched as Hakeem clipped the end with a practised motion, the scent of rich tobacco filling the air.

Lima noted the ritual with interest. *It was a flaw in Hakeem's armour which could be exploited.*

"I will need more notes next month," Lima told Hakeem.

"How much?"

"A crore," Lima said.

Hakeem turned around to look at his men. All of them seemed happy that their business was booming. "Can be done," Hakeem said.

"What'd you need from us?" Lima asked.

"Two weeks' notice. And 40 per cent advance."

Lima didn't flinch. "Of course," he said and then repeated Hakeem's words. "Trust is everything in this business."

Lima picked up the bag with the FICNs and the trio returned to their car in a manner that did not justify the rush in their hearts. Lima had won Hakeem's trust. And he would use that trust to push him over the edge. But before Hakeem could be dispatched, Lima had to destroy the currency notes he had obtained. There was no way they could let these notes enter the Indian market.

Later in the afternoon, Lima drove the vehicle towards the forest. Chad and Zoro had packed some camping gear in the boot of the car. They picked up bottles of alcohol along the way. After hours of driving, the vehicle juddered to a halt and its sputtering was swallowed by the dense symphony of the jungle. Fifty lakh ghosts of counterfeit rupees were pressing against Lima's backpack.

The clearing emerged. It was a hidden sanctuary beside a gurgling stream. They set up camp, flames flickering to life like defiant stars. Bottles were popped open. Cheers clinked. The bundles of notes were macabre offerings to the fire. Each bundle sent the fire hissing towards the sky. In the distance, a lone bird's call echoed, a mournful calling for Hakeem's death.

The trio returned to India after a painful but successful leg of their mission was accomplished. Across the dusty desk, Colonel Sobhraj, his sharp eyes momentarily dulled by fatigue, tapped a file against the blotter. But he returned to his bright self on sighting Agent Lima.

"The surveillance unit has heard whispers," Sobhraj said. "Hakeem's been chattering to his master, Lal Mohammad."

Colonel Sobhraj was amused. The lure of crores had finally lured Lal Mohammad out of his rathole. The elusive puppet master had finally appeared on the radar.

Sobhraj's hands were heavy with the gravity of countless silenced whispers. He pulled out a vial which was nestled in a drawer. Crystal clear, it held—death. Thallium Sulphate, the invisible killer, a favourite of secret service agencies since the Cold War. Odourless. Tasteless; a slow descent into the grave.

Lima's spine tingled. He remembered the lectures he had attended while learning with the Agency. His mind drifted to another investigation. Georgi Markov, a Bulgarian dissident, was a victim of Thallium's invisible kiss. The KGB had orchestrated his assassination with chilling precision. While waiting at a bus stop in London, a secret agent brushed past him, delivering the fatal dose via a modified umbrella tip. A tiny pellet embedded itself in Markov's leg, releasing Thallium into his bloodstream. The poison was subtle, undetectable until it was too late. It killed slowly, agonisingly, just as these counterfeit notes were designed to slowly bleed the economy.

Lima stared at the vial, a grim weapon of death.

"Make it look like God's will," Colonel Sobhraj said with finality. "Not ours."

***

The next month, Lima returned to Kathmandu along with Chad and Zoro to conclude the bigger deal worth one crore rupees with Hakeem. They stayed at a different hotel this time to avoid suspicion and the lethargy of a comfort zone. Getting too comfortable with the surroundings could be a death knell for an agent. On the other hand, awareness was Lima's lifeline and it would only heighten in a new dwelling, even if temporarily. Lima established contact with Hakeem over the telephone.

"I have the advance ready," Lima said.

"Very well," Hakeem said. "My boys will come to collect it."

"Hakeem bhai, we are partners now. We have bigger plans. They need bigger discussions."

"What do you need from me?"

"A meeting with your higher-ups," Lima said. "We'll pay the advance and discuss the next deal at the same time."

"Let me think it over," Hakeem said.

A couple of days later, Hakeem sent word to Lima that his *boss* was ready to meet them. Lima, Chad and Zoro were given an address and asked to show up within an hour. The trio got into their vehicle and drove to the point. After a few minutes of waiting, Hakeem's men arrived in a car.

One of them popped his head out of the window. "Follow us," he said.

Lima, who was good at high-speed driving, turned the steering wheel and began following them. They drove for about forty minutes until they arrived at the outskirts of Kathmandu, and stopped outside a huge cabin. The three didn't carry any weapons but Zoro had again taped the knife inside his shoe whereas Lima had taped two blades to the side of his mouth. There was no sense in bringing a sword to a gunfight, but this wasn't a gunfight; yet.

If things went awry, they could at least take hostages with their weapons and try to work their way out from there. Weapons were to be used as a last resort. Their main intention was to get a visual on Lal Mohammad; and eliminate both Lal Mohammad and Hakeem at a later point of time.

Sunlight pierced through dusty slats and illuminated motes in the stale air. Agent Lima, Chad and Zoro were patted down by Hakeem's men and then walked into the cabin. Armed men stood guard. The trio perched on rickety bamboo stools, backs pressed against the wall. Across from them, Hakeem exuded a predatory stillness.

Agent Lima placed a leather bag on the rough-hewn table. Crisp bills of forty lakhs. Genuine, courtesy of the RBI. He pushed the bag towards Hakeem. The henchman's thick fingers twitched. He lifted the bag, hefted it, then set it down with a thud that echoed in the cramped space.

"So you wanted to meet my boss?" Hakeem said, his voice rough as gravel.

Lima was unflinching. "Bigger fish, bigger pond."

"My boss doesn't deal with minnows."

"Minnows don't deal in crores, either."

Hakeem's smile was replaced by a glacial stare. An intangible tremor rippled through the room. Tension coiled. With a grunt, Hakeem rose and beckoned the agents with a grunt and a jerk of his head. They followed him through a maze of corridors. Each turn was a potential chokepoint. A lurking threat. Up the rickety stairs, past the watchful eyes, they climbed to the upper floor of the cabin.

Hakeem stopped before a heavy wooden door. He rapped twice. A rhythmic beat thrummed through Lima's chest. The door creaked open. Hakeem pushed it wide, gesturing for the agents to enter. Agent Lima moved. Chad and Zoro followed.

Inside, a lone figure sat silhouetted in a wooden armchair. On sighting Lima, the figure shifted. He was Lal Mohammad, the enigma. A thin smile played on his lips. Hakeem handed over the leather bag which he had carried to the big boss, who appeared pleased.

"Why this…need…to meet me?" Lal Mohammad said.

"Business partners should know each other," Lima said. "We've been dealing with Hakeem for a while. And wanted to pay our respects to those who should command it."

"Hakeem told me that you have bigger plans?"

"Oh, yes! The next deal is going to be massive."

"How much?"

Lima raised five fingers of his right hand. "Five crores."

"Good," Lal Mohammad said. "This calls for a celebration."

One of Hakeem's boys brought a tray with four glasses of shots and placed them on the table. Lima, Chad and Zoro had a thousand thoughts crossing their heads but they didn't exchange looks. Lal Mohammad picked up his glass.

"If I can trust your presence, will you not trust me with a drink?" Lal Mohammad said, sensing the hesitation of the three men. He raised his glass. "Cheers."

Sensing the challenge, Lima picked up his glass and downed it in a go. If something were to happen to him, Chad and Zoro would have time to respond. He felt the beverage slither down his throat, into the pit of his belly. For a moment, his heart was racing. And then there was nothing. Chad and Zoro also drank and a further discussion about the logistics of the current deal followed.

"You'll get the currency in two weeks," Lal Mohammad said.

Throughout all of this, Agent Lima subtly traced the map of Lal Mohammad's face: the cheekbones carved beneath his eyes. A tiny mole nestled at the corner of his lip. Lima committed every nuance to memory, a mental sketchpad for a meticulous rendition waiting back in Delhi. Finally, the Agency had a visual on Lal Mohammad. He was now a marked man.

***

The friendship between Lima and Hakeem had begun to grow. Lima went to great lengths to win Hakeem's trust, often dining out with him at great personal risk. When he was confident that Hakeem had stopped being suspicious about him, Lima called the man to a teahouse in Kathmandu on the pretext of paying the next instalment for the one crore rupee-deal.

Hakeem accepted the invitation and was on his way to meet Lima. The air was full of the cloying sweetness of yak butter tea in the teahouse. Outside, the cacophony of Kathmandu's Thamel district filtered through the thin window.

Agent Lima swirled the amber liquid in his cup. Metallic twangs reverberated each time his spoon touched the borders of the cup. Hakeem arrived in his vehicle, driven by his men. He asked his men to wait outside the teahouse while he discussed business with Lima.

"What is this, my man?" Hakeem said as he sat down. "A man should drink stronger stuff."

"I'll meet you at the bar in the evening," Lima said. "Until then, this drink is good enough."

"Neat place," Hakeem said, looking around.

"Do you want to order something?"

Hakeem's eyes narrowed, his gaze flicking to the ornate teapot resting on the low table. Lima tilted the teapot, the near-invisible flow of liquid adding another layer of sweat to his already clammy palms. His cup clinked against the saucer as he reached for it.

"No," Hakeem said.

Lima didn't react. He knew that Hakeem would be looking out for his insistence, and he didn't give him that at all.

"Fine," Lima said. "Here's the next instalment."

Agent Lima pushed the bag towards Hakeem. He watched, as Hakeem took a long, appreciative breath. Lima settled back into the cushions, the conversation flowing easily now, fuelled by greed.

"And to cement our friendship," Lima said, "here's something for you."

From his pocket, Lima pulled out a box of Cuban cigars. The box was completely sealed. Hakeem held the box, his fingers tracing the smooth edges, caressing the promise within. The scent of rich tobacco enveloped him. Each cigar, a masterpiece wrapped in the rustic embrace of Havana, was filled with the allure of indulgence. His eyes sparkled like a connoisseur savouring an elixir, that *harmless* box of Cuban cigars.

"Finally," Hakeem said, "a gift worthy of a man like me."

Lima nodded, acknowledging Hakeem's appreciation. Then the two shook hands and Hakeem lumbered out of the teahouse, leaving Lima with the remnants of their conversation and the eventual consequences of his actions. The aftertaste of the yak butter tea lingered in Lima's mouth, a reminder that the poison—Thallium Sulphate—had been delivered, smeared inside the cigars which had later been packed and sealed. Thallium was odourless. There was no way Hakeem would be able to figure out that each cigar had a lethal dose packed into the tobacco. Now Lima only had to wait for Hakeem to light his own pyre.

At his den, in the evening, Hakeem was enjoying his drink when he remembered about the cigars. He opened the packet and cradled the Havana cigar between his thumb and forefinger. Fat and smooth; the wrapper the colour of aged leather. He held the cigar to his nose, inhaling the complex aroma—earthy, sweet and with a hint of spice.

With a flick of his wrist, he sparked a lighter. The flame lit up like a miniature inferno. He brought the fire to the foot of the cigar. The first draw was a revelation—a rich, full-bodied wave washing over his palate. He closed his eyes and relished the ritual. In the haze of smoke, Hakeem felt *something*. He just didn't know *what*.

Three days later, Hakeem's world began to crumble. A metallic tang haunted his tongue, a grim echo of impending death. A dull throb crept into his limbs, sapping his strength. Kathmandu's doctors were baffled. No fever. No illness. Only a steady decline that defied diagnosis. Whispers of black magic or divine retribution followed. His voice, once booming, turned raspy. His mountain-like frame shrunk by unseen hands. In a sterile hospital room, stripped of his power, Hakeem turned into a hollow shell of his former self. His gaze landed on a crumpled napkin. That had been his fate.

Lal Mohammad had come down to meet his man on Friday. The doctors had made it clear that Hakeem didn't have long to live. For the first time in many years, Lal Mohammad felt a pinch of emotion. Hakeem's lips quivered. He was struggling to speak, staring at the ceiling, as if he had spotted the angel of death.

His trembling hand tried reaching for Lal Mohammad. He wanted to warn his boss with a single word. *Him,* he wanted to say, him. But darkness claimed him before the warning could be delivered. His eyes were shut. Forever.

But in the shadows, Agent Lima was pleased with his work. A grim satisfaction twisted his lips. The Delhi winter held Lima in its icy grip even within the cavernous Chandni Chowk Metro Station. His warm clothes offered much comfort against the biting wind whistling through the station's open-air platforms. The last metro for the night stopped smoothly. Doors parted open and Lima stepped inside the compartment. His eyes scanned the bogey and he saw Colonel Sobhraj seated at some distance. He had a newspaper in his hands. Lima took his seat beside the Colonel.

"Did they conduct a post-mortem on Hakeem?" Lima asked.

"No," Colonel Sobhraj said. "The cause of death is only mentioned as multiple organ failure. We took care of that."

"Good riddance."

"But the bigger one scurried away."

Lima frowned. "Lal Mohammad?"

"Yes. Gone off-grid. Typical."

Colonel Sobhraj produced a worn out photograph from the midst of the newspaper. It was a hand-drawn image of Lal Mohammad, eyes glinting with an unsettling intensity.

"Your intel is our best shot at tracing him," Colonel Sobhraj said.

"Have we dispatched more eyes to get sight of him?"

Colonel Sobhraj nodded. "The Agency *usually* claims its prey," he said. "Time will be his judge."

The metro screeched to a halt at the next station. The doors hissed open. Colonel Sobhraj stepped off, the cold air biting deeper. Agent Lima continued the journey forward. He had completed his mission, delivered a twisted form of justice but the victory tasted like ash. It would take eight long years before the win could be solidified.

***

September 2020: Late Monday evening, Lal Mohammad stepped out of his garment factory in Jambu Danda, Gothatar. The cool night air whispered through the narrow streets as he mounted his motorcycle with the number plate Ba 6 Cha 5152. The street lights created an eerie atmosphere. Lal Mohammad had become increasingly paranoid. He was convinced that secret service agents were out to kill him, constantly looking over his shoulder and avoiding routines.

Suddenly, the growl of a motorcycle engine pierced the silence. Two masked figures on a motorcycle sped towards him. Gunshots rang out, shattering the stillness. Lal Mohammad barely had time to react. Bullets struck his head, chest, and stomach. He swerved desperately, trying to avoid the onslaught but his efforts were in vain. The pain was immediate and excruciating as he collapsed onto the pavement, blood pooling around him.

The attackers fled, their figures disappearing into the night. Nearby CCTV cameras captured the entire scene, the grainy footage later revealing the brutal efficiency of the hit. Passersby, drawn by the commotion, rushed to his aid. They lifted his lifeless body and hurried him to the Shankarapur Hospital. Despite their efforts, the severity of his injuries required a transfer to the TU Teaching Hospital in Maharajganj, where doctors could do nothing more than declare him dead.

Nepal police swiftly closed all checkpoints. But the assailants had vanished without a trace. Lal Mohammad's death sent ripples through the intelligence community. Indian agencies had long sought him for his ties to Dawood Ibrahim and the ISI, linking him to anti-India activities and the flood of counterfeit currency.

"India had always been looking for him due to his associations," said an officer from Nepal's Special Bureau.

Back in Delhi, Colonel Sobhraj leaned back in his chair, a rare smile curling his lips. He stood up, walking over to the small bar in his office and selected a bottle of his finest single malt scotch. Pouring a generous measure into a crystal glass, he added a single ice cube, watching it clink and melt slightly. The soft glow of his desk lamp added a warm ambiance to the room. Colonel Sobhraj set the glass down, the liquid swirling gently. He watched; and allowed himself a rare moment of relaxation.

***

Palm leaves fluttered softly outside the restaurant in Juhu. The sea breeze wafted through the open windows, carrying the scent of salt and distant waves. Mr Zaidi and Lucky Bisht had finished their meal at a corner table. Mr Zaidi's eyes, sharp and inquisitive, contrasted with Lucky's calm, steady gaze—a gaze shaped by countless covert missions. Lucky leaned back, savouring the last bite of his grilled fish.

"So, Zaidi saab, where do we go from here?" he asked.

"You've taken me through quite a journey through the murky alleys of Kathmandu today," Mr Zaidi said.

"Lima's stories, just like the man, thrive in chaos."

"I'll be waiting to hear more," Mr Zaidi said.

Mr Zaidi paid the bill, and tipped the waiter well. As they exited the restaurant, the city lights flickered on, blending with the stars above. The soft hum of traffic and distant chatter of beachgoers filled the air. Neon signs glowed vibrantly, casting colourful reflections on the wet pavement. A movie hoarding was visible at the junction. Mr Zaidi and Lucky Bisht strolled along the promenade towards their vehicle, their steps in sync, waiting for the next chapter of Agent Lima's story to unfold.

two

Operation Jungle Safari

In the suburban heart of Mumbai, two men from different worlds found themselves in a perfectly lit study. The room, adorned with bookshelves holding countless volumes, was a sanctuary of stories. A large mahogany desk dominated the centre. On its surface were more books. Notes. Pens. Unpublished manuscripts. This room was where some of India's most famous crime novels had been written by none other than S. Hussain Zaidi, often referred to as the number one writer in the crime genre in India.

Mr Zaidi sat in a high-backed chair. His keen eyes, behind rimmed glasses, glinted with curiosity and intellect. Across from him sat Lucky Bisht—the silent sentinel, former commando of the NSG and bearer of countless untold tales.

"Zaidi saab," Lucky said, "you have delved into the nooks of this city and uncovered many secrets. But there are tales of valour and sacrifice that lie buried in the jungles far from here."

Mr Zaidi looked up, intrigued. "Where did these happenings take place?"

Lucky's gaze turned distant, as if seeing through the walls of the study to far-off lands. He was transported to the dense forests of Nagaland, to a time where militancy was at its peak, when the sound of gunfire and the scent of gunpowder hung heavy in the air.

"Okay then," Mr Zaidi said. "Take me to the heart of this faraway jungle, to those moments and the man who defined this mission."

***

2007: The shrieking klaxon echoed through the corrugated metal roof of the Army Battalion HQ, shattering the pre-dawn silence of Phek district, Nagaland. Agent Lima's muscles scrambled with haste under the effects of sleep. His mind snapped to attention, instincts honed by countless nights of training.

Sleep deprivation had been a relentless drill in his training days. Instructors would force them to stay awake for days, testing their endurance, breaking them down to rebuild them stronger. Lima recalled the harsh lights of the training camp, the barking commands, the constant push to keep moving. Sleep was a luxury he'd learned to do without.

His body responded with a precision born from those gruelling sessions. Eyes bleary but focused, he shoved off the thin blanket and swung his legs off the cot. His feet hit the cold floor with a thud. The fog of sleep cleared quickly, replaced by the sharp clarity of mission mode. He was hearing sounds of gunfire.

The spartan room was lit by a single bulb and bore the telltale signs of a temporary existence—crumpled maps sprawled across a cot and half-empty mugs abandoned on the table. Agent Lima's eyes caught sight of Lt Dogra's unpacked duffel which was spewing clothes across the floor. Across the room, Dogra rummaged frantically through a drawer. He was a fresh-faced lieutenant from the Indian Military Academy in Dehradun and posted to the Northeast. His fingers clawed through with urgency.

The window was framed by a pale white mosquito netting. Lima caught a glimpse of the pre-dawn landscape—rolling hills cloaked in mist and the silhouettes of distant palm trees swaying against the sky. Serenity was the greatest cloak of the Northeast and hid a simmering tension underneath. Lima listened. Distant, muffled explosions and the staccato crackle of gunfire. He ran to the window. A ghastly sight awaited him.

"KYKL militants have sieged the police station!" Lima shouted.

Lt Dogra resurfaced, in full gear. He was raring to go after finding what he had been looking for in the drawer—a ring. He triumphantly held aloft a ring adorned in the shape of a horseshoe. Dogra slipped the ring on and it laced his voice with confidence.

"My lucky charm," he said. "Can't leave it behind."

Lima shook his head. *Mystical defence system against bullets.* His shoulders were heavy with the reality of experience. He knew better than to argue with the greenhorn's faith. Dogra viewed the world through idealistic glasses. The war was yet to etch its harsh realities onto his soul. Besides, faith was not a bad thing; not at all. Faith often kept men going in adverse circumstances. Dogra was one amongst them.

Lima grabbed his tactical vest from the back of a chair. Strapping it on, he tightened each buckle, ensuring a snug fit. His fingers moved to the utility belt, fastening it around his waist, securing his pistol and extra magazines. He pulled on his combat boots, lacing them tightly, and grabbed his helmet, slipping it over his head. Each piece of gear felt like an extension of his body.

With one final check of his equipment, Lima was ready. "Let's go," he said.

The duo sprinted for the Gypsy which was parked under the skeletal glow of a lamp. Lima took the wheel and began driving until the air went thick with the acrid tang of gunpowder. Dogra's eyes kept darting between the distant flashes of gunfire. Then, there was movement in the air—a wave of energy coming towards them.

"Incoming," Dogra shrieked.

Boom! A grenade exploded. Shockwaves rocked the vehicle. Lima dived out of the vehicle with fluidity but Dogra hesitated for a crucial moment. Then, with a scream torn from his throat, he followed suit and landed heavily beside Lima on the dew-kissed grass. He groaned and clutched his hand. His face contorted in pain. Lima clamped a hand over his buddy's mouth.

"Shhh!" Lima hissed. "We'll draw fire."

Dogra's eyes widened with a dawning horror. When he held up his hand, his ring finger was gone. A bloody, mangled stub remained. The lucky horseshoe ring was grotesquely jammed onto the jeep frame where he'd grabbed for support. The weight of his dive, combined with the cumbersome equipment, had ripped it clean off. His supposed talisman had failed him miserably. The irony was too much for Lima to bear.

The duo held position until more units responded. Gunfire subsided and was finally replaced by the wail of sirens from ambulances and fire brigades. The militants were pushed back. Dogra was bundled into an ambulance. His mangled hand and shattered faith in lucky charms was now covered by a sterile, white sheet.

As the dust settled, Lima thought about the shape of the horseshoe. It was a reminder etched in metal. War, he was perfectly aware, couldn't be fought with trinkets. To fight a war, one needed an ice-cold heart. Sharp mind. Steely resolve. An ability to deal with loss. He watched the ambulance disappear into the distance. A heavy sigh escaped his lips.

Lima returned to the base and returned his equipment to the Keeper of Technical Equipment (KOTE) in a highly secure room where military equipment like night vision goggles, compass and weapons were stored. KOTE typically referred to the individual responsible for managing, maintaining and distributing technical gear and tools in a military setting. This person ensures that all technical equipment is operational, correctly calibrated and ready for use.

After depositing the equipment, Lima returned to his room. The rising sun had cast an orange glow on the distant hills. The beauty was macabre, almost. Unlike the idyllic landscapes on postcards, this war gave absolutely *zero fucks* to lucky charms or second chances. The conflict driving the war was deeply rooted in the region's history.

The Northeast of India had a long and complex history of insurgency, marked by ethnic strife, demands for autonomy and militant movements. This region, rich in cultural diversity, had seen numerous insurgent groups rise and fall. Among these, the Kanglei Yawol Kanna Lup (KYKL) stood out as a significant force. It was formed in January 1994 by a faction of the United National Liberation Front (UNLF) led by Namoijam Oken in conjunction with splinter groups of Kangleipak Communist Party (KCP) and People's Revolutionary Party of Kangleipak (PREPAK).

The KYKL, primarily comprising the Meitei ethnic group, sought sovereignty for the entire northeastern region, resisting Indian state control. Their operations were marked by guerrilla tactics, surprise attacks, and efforts to blend with the civilian population, making them a persistent challenge for Indian security forces. The group's influence and activities underscored the deep-seated tensions and the ongoing struggle for identity and autonomy in the northeast. It was these KYKL militants who had attacked the police station. And the Indian Army knew that a swift and strong retribution would be the only deterrent to such attacks in the future.

***

In his cabin, Colonel Sobhraj was thinking; and that is when he was most dangerous. Promoted barely a year ago, his rise had been swift, fuelled by a reputation for ruthless efficiency. The insignia on his collar gleamed as a reminder of the trust his superiors had vested upon him.

Colonel Sobhraj surveyed the aftermath with cold, calculating eyes. The attack on the police station was more than a militant strike; it was a direct affront to India's sovereignty. He knew the response had to be swift and unyielding. Plans were already forming in his mind. He would strike back quickly to send a clear message that such aggression would be met with cold, deadly and overwhelming retribution.

Colonel Sobhraj's eyes scanned the maps spread across his desk. Each line and contour held a secret, a potential move in the intricate game of warfare. The officer was renowned for his piercing stare gaze that could strip a man in seconds. Tactical brilliance defined him. From his gold medal at the National Defence Academy to his service in Siachen, the legend of Sobhraj was etched not in his victories alone but in the silence of a particular night in Kashmir.

During an unforgiving blizzard, where visibility was nil, Sobhraj had disappeared for hours, only to return with crucial intel that turned the tide of an entire campaign. His survival was a mystery. Frostbite had seared patterns into his skin but his spirit had remained unbroken. His meticulous routine, the way he held his gun—were all a subtle display of his military brilliance.

Now in the silence of his cabin, Sobhraj's thoughts took form. Unusual humidity seemed to fuel a rage within him. The militants had dared to attack the police station, an emblem of the state. They'd pay for their actions.

Agent Lima was also present in the cabin with a mysterious man who had covered his face with a *gamcha*. This man was an informant named "*Pakki Khabar*". His face was shrouded to guard his anonymity. Pakki Khabar was renowned for his flawless intel which had led to the capture or surrender of many militants in the past. This time, he had brought news about some militants, who were involved in the attack on the police station, hiding in a distant village.

"How many?" Colonel Sobhraj asked.

"Seven," Pakki Khabar's voice rasped. "They've slipped in with the civilians, using them as shields."

"Guerrilla tactics," Sobhraj said. "Hit and run. And then hide amongst their own."

Sobhraj rested his palm on the wooden table, betraying the storm within. Finally, his voice cut through the tension, tight with fury.

"Let's get those bastards," Colonel Sobhraj said. "Lima will lead a seven-man team to find and neutralise them. Return before dawn. No collateral damage. Clear?"

Lima's stomach churned. This wasn't the surgical strike he craved, the clean takedown with minimal casualties. This was going to be a Cordon and Search Operation. This was about finding the guilty hidden amongst the innocent under the cloak of night. Each decision from now would be a walk on the tightrope between justice and brutality. Lima met Pakki Khabar's gaze with an unsettling coldness. In the flickering light, Lima saw not just an informant but a reflection of the moral compass that would guide them; for better or worse.

Tension crackled as the team geared up. The room buzzed with the rustle of tactical vests and the metallic clicks of weapons being loaded. Lima slipped into his camouflaged Kevlar vest, securing it tightly. It was equipped with reinforced plates capable of stopping high-calibre rounds. He fastened his utility belt, laden with grenades, extra magazines and a kukri with its curved blade glinting ominously.

The forward-curving blade, about a foot long, was perfect for close combat and cutting through dense jungle foliage. The handle was carved from dark hardwood and fitted perfectly into Lima's grip. It had brass inlays and a small notch at the base of the blade, a traditional design element.

The rest of the team also geared up. Night vision goggles. Submachine guns. Assault rifles. Each soldier donned lightweight tactical gloves and knee pads, designed for mobility and protection. The map unfolded like a silent blueprint for their hunt.

The team believed it'd be quick, a few hours. But Lima was aware of the grim realities. Nothing took a few hours. If things went SNAFU (situation normal, all f**ked up!)—it could take them days to return to their base. By the time the seven-man team finished their grim preparations, the clock had ticked past 10:30 pm. *Operation Jungle Safari had begun.*

The air outside felt colder than usual as Lima led the team away from the camp's relative safety and ventured into the vast, looming forest. Darkness clung to the trees like a second skin and swallowed the light with hesitant glances. They moved in single file. The order was meticulously planned by Lima. Rakesh, a seasoned soldier, led the way, his silhouette swallowed by the darkness ahead. Lima was behind the pointman and followed by others. Pakki Khabar—the shrouded informant—stuck close to Lima, and he was supposed to be protected for only he knew the hideout of the militants. Next to him walked Jeevan Deka, each man seeing only the fleeting glimpse of the one before him.

Colonel Sobhraj's orders were clear as crystal: maintain radio silence, preserve secrecy above all else. No artificial light would pierce the inky night, no easy path cleared by villagers would be used in their approach. Treaded paths in the jungles were prone to dangers. They were fighting a guerilla army who knew more than a thing or two about taking advantage of the topography. Militants would often lay booby traps on the routes that the Army was known to take to reach the villages.

Lima remembered a soldier had fallen into the pit and lost a pound of flesh to punji traps. These were simple yet effective booby traps consisting of camouflaged pits dug into the ground and lined with sharpened bamboo stakes. Often covered with foliage or other materials, these traps were designed to injure or impale unsuspecting soldiers who stumbled into them.

Lima forced the team to push through thickets of overgrown grass and thorny bushes. The muddy path was damp and treacherous underfoot. Faint crackles of the walkie-talkie held tightly by the radioman was their only lifeline to connectivity. The forest stretched around them; a silent ocean whispering unseen dangers. Crickets chirped. The snap of a twig or rustle of leaves sent shivers down several spines. The jungle could be unforgiving. Of this, Lima was perfectly aware.

Lima held his assault rifle, a Kalashnikov, closer to his hips in a low-ready position. It offered better manoeuvrability when squeezing through tight spaces. His dominant right hand maintained a firm grip while the non-dominant hand supported the magazine. Lima's breath was shallow but controlled. The weapon felt cold and heavy in his hands, a reminder of the violence about to come. He kept stepping forward. What else was there to do?

The journey was still some way to go even after three hours into the humid slog. Lima turned to catch a glimpse of Pakki Khabar. The man was safe, a package that had to be protected at all costs. He was wary of the jungle for it held dark secrets in its dense foliage. Just paces further, a rustle in the undergrowth startled Agent Lima. The pointman squinted against the oppressive darkness. A silhouette emerged. Strange. They were still kilometres from the hideout of the militants. Pangs of surprise snaked through Lima's gut. *Who the fuck was that?*

***

For a heartbeat, Lima hoped it was a villager who had fallen into their path. The figure shifted. The faint starlight caught a glint of metal. A large rifle materialised, aimed straight at Lima. Before he could react, the night erupted. Three deafening cracks split the silence. Bullets whizzed past Lima's ear. He hit the dirt, and felt his heart pounding inside the cage of his ribs. Chaos. Absolute chaos. The men in the front returned fire. Lima's rifle spat bullets and the rest of the team scrambled for cover. Darkness made it impossible for the men in the rear to fire. There was no way for them to know if someone friendly was in their line of fire.

Lima analysed that the militants had changed their position and moved from their original hideout to the forest. The unseen enemy traded bursts every few minutes. It was less about killing, more about holding ground. The enemy's gunfire was heavier and had pinned Lima and his team down. Lima was wondering if the radio man had called for backup. But it was impossible to know in the pitch dark of the night. Lima looked around and saw…nothing.

All he could do was wait for dawn to arrive. Lima held ground the entire night. No one could speak a word for the fear of revealing their positions. The arrival of dawn was slow and agonising but finally revealed the night's grisly toll. At the break of light, Lima wondered about Pakki Khabar's fate; the prime package who was supposed to be protected somehow. Where was the man?

Still in a prone position, Agent Lima caught something gaping at him. *Damn.* He shook his head to make sure of what he was seeing. Then he gulped. Pakki Khabar's eyes, still attached to his head, were staring at Lima. The head had been severed from the torso. Pakki Khabar had taken the full impact of the initial burst of the enemy and dropped dead.

Lima then wondered about the reinforcements. They hadn't arrived throughout the night. How could they? The radioman was dead too, sprawled against a tree. A coincidence had trapped them. In the jungle, the hunter had turned into prey. The break of light gave them some relief. Most of the militants had fallen back into the villages. But there was one who was heavily injured and had been left behind. Lima and the team decided to flank him.

In the foliage of the northeast, a tableau of conflict unfolded as Lima and his team moved closer to one of the insurgents responsible for Pakki Khabar's death. The man, injured and defeated, lay beside his M-16 rifle—a weapon known for its reliability and widespread use in conflicts across the world.

The M-16 rifle, a gas-operated, air-cooled weapon firing 5.56×45mm cartridges, was renowned for its accuracy and reliability. Lightweight and low-recoil, it had a high cyclic rate of fire, making it effective at ranges up to 550 metres. Yet it lay discarded, its owner incapacitated by wounds. The insurgent was clad in a patchwork of civilian clothes and a makeshift camouflage vest.

Lima approached the militant, his own weapon—an AK-47—poised and ready. The AK-47, with its distinctive silhouette and 7.62mm rounds, was a contrast to the insurgent's M-16. The M-16 was a more advanced rifle in terms of fire rate. But Lima's weapon held the upper hand right now.

"Where are the others?" Lima asked the man who had been left behind.

The insurgent's grunts were met with Lima's unwavering resolve. The conversation between Lima and the informant, a terse exchange of demands resulted in a deadlock. The militant was bleeding from his mouth. He refused to buckle to Lima's demands and tried to move towards his rifle. His movements were slow, and painful. Agent Lima noticed this and fired a single burst from his rifle to end the agony of the insurgent's existing wounds. The AK-47 ended the insurgent's life in a brief, brutal moment. The rest of the unit looked on.

Retrieving the military-grade walkie-talkie from the radioman's remains, Lima keyed in the frequency for direct communication with Colonel Sobhraj. The walkie-talkie, designed for rugged use and secure lines, crackled to life as Lima reported the grim outcome. His voice remained steady through the radio static.

"Sir, Pakki Khabar is dead," he said. "I repeat, Pakki Khabar is dead."

Colonel Sobhraj's response was immediate, a low rumble over the secure channel. "Understood, Lima. Reinforcements and supplies are en route. Continue the cordon and search operation. We'll flush them out."

The arrival of army trucks marked the next phase of their mission. Lima, with methodical precision, distributed the supplies among his team. There was a trail which the militants had left behind. And Lima was going to follow them. The military-grade compass and detailed map, essential tools for their navigation, were entrusted to Deka and Rakesh. Their purpose was clear: to delve into the heart of the village, dismantle the insurgent threat, and secure a victory for the army in the northeast.

***

Through the jungles, Lima and his unit navigated the delicate balance between vigilance and the necessity of their mission. The jungle was a living entity. And soldiers were aware of its dangers. They didn't fear the terrain but respected it as a friend, and foe.

The region was a mosaic of indigenous cultures and natural beauty. Scars of a protracted insurgency had not only stalled progress but also deeply divided its people.

Agent Lima had also undergone rigorous training at the Counter-Insurgency and Jungle Warfare School in Mizoram to train in a challenging environment that mimicked the conditions of real conflict zones. He'd honed his skills in guerrilla tactics, survival and navigation. Daily drills had pushed him to his physical and mental limits, instilling in him the resilience needed to operate effectively in hostile environments. This intensive preparation was pivotal in shaping him into the proficient soldier he was today, adept at navigating the nuances of warfare in the jungle.

Lima's unit was following the trail into the outskirts of the village. The trek and the constant threat of ambush had wearied them. The sight of a farmer momentarily heightened Lima's apprehension. Their last encounter with militants, a harrowing ambush that had left them on edge had coloured his perception of every human form. The serene picture of the farmer who was engrossed in his daily routine clashed with Lima's heightened alertness. The farmer also noticed the disturbance and turned out to find himself surrounded by a posse of ghost-like soldiers whose posturing made them appear like angels of death.

"Anyone passed through here?" Lima asked.

"Just the usual," the farmer replied.

The simplicity of the question and the answer belied the complex web of suspicion and necessity in which Lima was entangled. The farmer, his life upended by the endless conflict, was a symbol of the civilian populace caught between opposing forces. The man's response was laced with the fatigue of someone who longed for nothing more than to tend to his flock of livestock in peace.

The unit, their instincts honed by the ambush, scrutinised the

The solution came from a deep asset in Bangladesh by the name of Mohammad Akram. A deep asset is an intelligence term referring to an operative who is deeply embedded within a target organisation or enemy territory. These operatives have established a significant cover identity, often over an extended period. Their deep integration allows them to access highly sensitive information and influence key events from within.

Akram had been propped up by the Agency in Bangladesh for several years, even decades. He had a flourishing scrap iron business which the Agency had helped set up. It was his front. He had connections with the elite, the police and the military and often provided the Agency with invaluable intel. During the time when the Agency was looking for Qureshi, Akram contacted the Agency with crucial information.

"I know where Qureshi operates," he had said. "But rare information comes for a rare price."

Akram's quote was one crore and seventy-five lakh rupees. The Agency, realising the gravity of the situation, agreed. They transferred half the amount upfront, with the promise of the rest upon confirmation of Qureshi's location. Two agents named Gamma and Charlie were selected for the mission. Gamma, a former military man, had a keen strategic mind and nerves of steel. Charlie was a surveillance expert picked up from the Indian Engineering Services. The duo was dispatched to Dhaka and Akram provided them with regular updates on Qureshi's movements.

"He's landing in Dhaka on Wednesday," Akram informed them during a secret meeting.

Gamma and Charlie got ready to execute the hit on Akram. On the night of the operation, the duo arrived at the location which Akram had provided to them—an abandoned paper factory which was eerily silent. Gamma checked his watch. It was time. They moved in, their training guiding every step.

Minutes turned into hours. And still, no sign of Qureshi. The uneasy silence was broken by the sudden appearance of ISI agents. Gamma and Charlie reacted instantly but they were outnumbered. Gamma fought fiercely; his military training evident in every move. Charlie used his agility to evade, to strike where least expected. But the ISI had come prepared.

Bound and gagged, they were dragged to an abandoned factory. The place was a grim reflection of their predicament. The interrogation began. Gamma endured the pain, his eyes defiant. Charlie, though tortured, never lost his wit, trying to buy time, to find a way out. But the ISI was relentless. Sensing their capability to withstand torture, the duo was mercilessly executed.

Akram, far away from the scene of betrayal, was already enjoying his rewards from the ISI. But his conscience was not silent. The faces of Gamma and Charlie haunted him, a reminder of his treachery. He tried to drown his guilt in more vices, but it only grew stronger. But why had Akram betrayed the organisation which had propped him up?

The answer lay in his vices. The iron business had made him wealthy, and gambling became his downfall. Losses piled up, and in desperation, he turned to the ISI. They offered him a deal: betray the Agency, and his debts would vanish. Akram agreed, leading Gamma and Charlie into a deadly trap.

Akram's dual life as an Agency asset and ISI informant was precarious. The ISI rewarded him but he was always looking over his shoulder. For the Agency, the loss was a call to action. Gamma and Charlie's deaths were not just a blow to their operations but a personal affront. Operation Tiger Claw was about avenging their fallen operatives. The hunt for Akram was on.

***

Later that month, Agent Lima and another operative known as Chad were headed for Darbhanga in Bihar. The two had worked together on several missions. On the journey, they shared cups of tea and the occasional cigarette when the train would halt at railway stations at midnight.

But before boarding the train to Bihar, Lima had also completed fourteen days of training at Leimakhong in Manipur under Colonel Sobhraj's command. He had been subjected to a battery of psychological tests by none other than the mastermind, the Phantom—Colonel Sobhraj.

Lima had sat in the interrogation room, the hum of the fluorescent lights echoing in the silence. The walls were a sterile white, the air heavy with anticipation. A single metal chair faced him, occupied by Colonel Sobhraj. The cold metal of the table pressed against Lima's arms, grounding him. There was a psychologist in the room, clipboard in one hand.

"Lion or fox?" the psychologist asked.

"Chameleon."

"Fire or ice?"

"Mist; enveloping, unseen."

Colonel Sobhraj took a step closer. "Do you feel fear, Lima?"

"Only if I let it in."

"Good." Sobhraj studied him, then nodded slowly. "Fear keeps you alive."

On the fifteenth day, Lima was once again standing in front of Colonel Sobhraj, waiting to receive instructions for his next mission. After asking Lima to sit, Colonel Sobhraj gave him a photograph of Akram and a context of the mission.

"He seems to be protected by the ISI," Colonel Sobhraj said. "We *cannot* let him get away."

Colonel Sobhraj's father had worked for the Ministry of Railways. His father would often tell him stories of the Rajdhani train which travelled Mumbai and Delhi. The train would usually run on time and a six-year-old Sobhraj had often heard his father say—the train *cannot* be late. The timings of the train were monitored directly from New Delhi. So Sobhraj had learnt from his father that some causes were non-negotiable.

Colonel Sobhraj had applied the same principles to Operation Tiger Claw and dispatched Lima and Chad towards Bangladesh. The mission was named as such because the Bengal tiger was the national animal of India and Bangladesh both. It suggested a powerful and decisive action, aligning well with the covert nature of the mission.

Lima and Chad stayed in Darbhanga for a few days to come up with a plan to cross the border. It is said that the name of the places derived from DwarBanga, which meant "gateway to Bangladesh". The total length of the border between Indian and Bangladesh was 4,096.7 km and was highly porous at that point of time. Only parts of this border were covered with physical fencing. The area was heavily patrolled by the Border Security Force (BSF) of India and the Bangladesh Rifles (BDR).

Bangladesh, formerly East Pakistan, had gained independence from Pakistan in 1971 after a brutal war of liberation in which India had played the role of a liberator. The BDR was established to secure the nation's borders. However, conflicts arose between the BDR and the BSF of India, primarily over issues of illegal migration, smuggling, and territorial disputes. These tensions occasionally flared into violent skirmishes, straining relations between the two neighbours.

In the cover of the night, a local contact led Lima and Chad to a point in the jungles and dropped them off. "Keep going straight until you reach the village," he said, and then turned around to return to safety.

Agent Lima and his associate, Chad, moved like ghosts through the dense thicket along the border, shrouded in the cover of darkness. The silence of their soft-soled shoes was occasionally disturbed by the rustling leaves and the distant hum of crickets. Lima, a figure clad in black, remained alert to every subtle shift in the surroundings. Behind him, Chad followed suit. He was equally adept at the clandestine arts.

"Where are we?" Chad asked in the midst of their journey.

Lima shrugged. "Keep going straight." *Who the fuck knew?*

The border was a mere line on the ground, invisible in the obscurity of the night. Silence enveloped them as they navigated the unfamiliar terrain. Occasional glimmers of moonlight guided them. The thrill of the illicit journey pulsed through their veins until they saw the lights of the houses in the village. The village, once an abstract notion, was now tangible beneath their feet. It marked the completion of a perilous milestone of the mission. As per orders from Sobhraj, Lima and Chad proceeded towards a house whose owner then led them to a waiting car which sped off from the inroads towards the national highway.

"How long until we reach Dhaka?" Lima asked the driver.

"Gyorah gha-a-nta lagegaa," the driver said, in his Bengali accent, indicating eleven hours.

"Get some rest," Chad told Lima.

It was a tactical understanding that only one of them would sleep at a time while the other would stay awake and alert. Though the driver had been arranged by the Agency, the deaths of Charlie and Gamma were a reminder for Lima that it was impossible to tell which friend would turn into a foe for the lure of minted currency notes. Lima pulled his cap over his head and rested the curve of his skull on the backrest of the seat. He slept until it was time to repay Chad's favour and stand guard for him.

In Dhaka, the duo checked into a low-scale motel named Golden Inn. Lima had been advised to choose low-scale hotels to stay on such missions as people usually minded their own business at such places. Lima and Chad had only carried a few clothes but had no weapons on their person. As was pre-decided, Lima got in touch with an operative named Victor over the satellite phone and informed him of his place of stay.

"Stay put," Victor told Lima. "A surprise guest will visit you in the evening."

Agent Lima and Chad spent most of the day watching television and waiting for the guest to arrive. The air in the motel room was heavy with the scent of discretion when there was a knock on the door in the evening. Lima opened the door just enough to take a peek at the guest's face. He was convinced by the man's looks that he had indeed been sent by Victor.

"The name's Khan," the man said. "Johnny Khan."

Lima rolled his eyes, convinced that the aspiring Bond's name was a lie but he had no interest in contesting it. The man was here to do a job which was more important than his identity. In this game of spies, everyone wore a mask. Some were funnier than the others.

Lima had put on his game face, grim and serious, whereas Johnny seemed like a jovial man with a paunch. Johnny Khan adjusted the brim of the NY Yankees cap on his head, approached the bed where Chad was sitting upright and placed a small package between him and Chad.

"Tools for the handymen," he said. "Very useful."

Lima unwrapped the package to reveal a local SIM card. A nondescript feature phone. Two sleek Star pistols, China made. All of this was nestled in foam padding. Bullets were placed in pouches. Chad inserted the SIM into the phone and switched it on, whereas Lima racked the pistol a couple of times to convince himself that the Chinese *maal* would work when it was needed the most. He remembered a saying which was common in Indian markets which were flooded with Chinese goods. *China ka maal, chala toh chand tak, nahi toh shaam tak.* There was no guarantee of Chinese goods. If they worked, they'd work forever. Or they could malfunction by the evening.

Lima's gaze bore into Johnny. It seemed like the man wanted to talk to them more, to increase his self-worth in the scheme of things. But as far as Lima was concerned, this conversation was over. Johnny appeared a little miffed that Lima hadn't turned out as friendly as he'd want.

Johnny retreated into the crowded streets of Dhaka. Lima and Chad were left in the company of the tools of this clandestine trade. The next morning, Lima and Chad began hustling for a new room for their stay. As per the information shared by the Agency, Akram was now living in an apartment which was close to the Army area. After reaching Road No. 4, where Akram was known to have purchased a new house, they learned that it was a high-end colony that was mostly occupied by high-ranking officials of the Army. Their first task was to identify the house where Akram was staying.

"The ISI has put him in bed with the BDR," Lima said to Chad, reflecting on the type of area he had taken up his residence in.

That was true. It was not that easy to procure a place in the Army area unless one had good *connections*. This fact was amply demonstrated by the amount of hustle they had to put in before they could get an apartment on rent on the first floor of a private bungalow. It was owned by an elderly married couple who lived on the ground floor. Rehman, an avuncular figure who was a big-time fan of old Bollywood songs and dialogues, was delighted to find visitors from India and hastily took them in as tenants.

"Bhare sawan mein registan lagta hai," Rehman said with a flourish as he took Lima's hand in his to shake it, "ye ghar mujhe khali makaan lagta hai."

Lima wasn't a Bollywood enthusiast. He could use his hands to count the total number of movies he had watched up until that point and would end up with at least a couple of fingers to spare. A fact that didn't help him at all in realising that Rehman was declaiming a dialogue from the 1997 movie *Naseeb,* in which a lovelorn and inebriated Govinda delivers the dialogue to his companion and benefactor Kader Khan. Lima had nothing but a smile to offer in return.

Uncle's excitement did not allow him to let go of Lima's hand as he kept jerking it up and down in a prolonged handshake. Chad stretched his hand forward. Uncle moved forward excitedly to shake hands with Chad.

"Keys?" Chad said wryly.

Uncle looked at him in surprise, his hand stopping in its tracks. Chad's poker face made him realise that his Bollywood theatrics had been going on for rather too long and he needed to hand them the keys to their newly rented apartment.

"There you go," Uncle said as he rummaged in his pocket for the keys. "Ek dum jhakaas!"

Chad and Lima climbed the narrow stairs to the first floor, the worn wooden boards creaking. Uncle's voice droned on behind them, a constant stream of filmy dialogues. Chad exchanged a weary glance with Lima, both silently grateful when they finally reached the landing. The door to their new apartment loomed ahead, a welcome escape from Uncle's endless small talk.

"I'll fire a bullet up his ass if he *jhakaas-es* me once again," Lima told Chad, and they both burst out laughing.

***

Lima and Chad needed to get some kind of employment to make their act look convincing. Their chosen profession also needed to allow them to scour the area, so that they could discover Akram's residence, without people getting too suspicious. Lima came up with the idea that they should enter the cable TV business. Lima stared out of the dusty window, the cityscape of Dhaka sprawling before him. The humid air, thick with the smell of fried snacks and diesel, was stifling. The streets were alive with a chaotic symphony of rickshaws, buses and street vendors. He turned to Chad, who was fiddling with a map.

"We need a way to move around without drawing attention," Lima said. "Akram's house won't find itself."

Chad glanced up, his eyes thoughtful. "I've been thinking. Cable TV operators. We can pose as them. They go everywhere, no one questions them."

"Good idea. The cable TV business here is booming. Perfect cover."

The cable TV industry in the subcontinent was indeed flourishing. Over 80 million subscribers across India and Bangladesh craved their daily dose of news, Bollywood films, and cricket. In Bangladesh alone, subscriptions had nearly doubled in recent years. People were eager to access new channels and stay connected to the world.

Lima leaned back in his chair, the gears turning in his mind. "So, we become operators. Get the gear, the uniforms. We'll need to learn their language too."

Chad nodded. "I can handle that. Worked with tech stuff before. How hard can it be? We can offer to upgrade their setups, check signal strength, whatever. That gives us an excuse to check each house."

"Right," Lima said, a plan forming. "We focus on the neighbourhoods Akram is likely to be in. Wealthy enough to afford cable, but not so upscale they'd have tight security."

Chad stood up, stretching his limbs. "Let's get to it then. I'll ask Victor to set up a deal with the local cable distributor."

Victor, their local contact, worked to get a meeting arranged with the local distributor. Lima and Chad left for their room for the meeting and blended into the streets below. The city was a labyrinth but now they had a thread to follow. As they walked, Lima felt a sliver of hope. This plan might just work. They could move unnoticed and find Akram without raising any alarm. Dhaka was unpredictable, a city of contrasts where the old met the new. But amidst the chaos, Lima and Chad had found their path. As cable TV operators, they would scour the area, inching closer to Akram's hideout with each visit. The game was on, and they were ready to play.

The cable operator was a portly man in his mid-forties. The duo met him at his office and offered to take over the operations of the area where Akram was suspectedly living. Chad made an elaborate pitch to the guy, detailing his plan to provide high-end set top boxes to the customers in the area. "If the pilot is successful, we plan to introduce an Android-based set top box which can also provide IPTV for the customers."

The concept of Internet Protocol Television (IPTV) began to take shape in the early 1990s. The idea was to use the internet to deliver TV content, a revolutionary shift from traditional broadcast methods. The cable guy was initially hesitant to hand over a franchise in an area he had dominated. But Lima and Chad started negotiating with him. The Agency had given them an approval of two and a half lakh takas for taking over the cable dealership.

"Two lakh takas as a one-time payment," Lima offered at the end of Chad's speech. "And 10 per cent royalty month on month."

"You must be joking!" the cable guy said. "Nothing less than four lakhs. And 20 per cent royalty."

Lima and Chad stared at each other. The cable guy's greed had left them astonished. The man was also measuring them, and after a while he seemed to have assessed that the duo did not have enough financial prowess. He stood up to leave. Lima had to make a quick decision.

"Three lakh takas," Lima said.

The cable operator did the math in his head. The upfront offer was good enough to cover him for a few years, at least.

"Done," he said.

"And 15 per cent royalty," Chad added.

The dealer agreed. Chad brought out the two and a half lakh takas which the Agency had delivered to them through Johnny. The man painstakingly counted each note. Lima promised to deliver the fifty thousand takas on the day when the man would formally hand over the business to them, which was going to be in the next two or three days. The man left happy, thinking that he had won the round of negotiation.

"Let him think that way," Lima told Chad. "We have bigger fish to fry."

Colonel Sobhraj knew it wasn't the best of scenarios when he heard that Lima had spent an additional fifty thousand takas to take over the business than what had been approved. The mission was already running over-budget. But Sobhraj had worked in the field and understood that operational decisions came at a cost and sometimes that cost would exceed the limits set by a bureaucrat who'd been sitting in his office. Explanations would have to be given, but he decided to cross that bridge when he came to it. Colonel Sobhraj agreed to transfer the extra money when Lima made another demand.

As he processed the request, Sobhraj's mind wandered to Operation Jawbreaker, a CIA mission that had similarly spiralled over-budget but ultimately proved successful. Following the 9/11 attacks, the CIA had launched this covert operation to coordinate with the Northern Alliance in Afghanistan and overthrow the Taliban regime.

Initial estimates had pegged the costs within manageable limits, but the reality on the ground demanded much more. Helicopter transports, cash payments to local warlords and unforeseen logistical challenges had all contributed to the budget overruns.

Despite the financial strain, Operation Jawbreaker succeeded beyond expectations. Gary Schroen, a veteran CIA officer, had led the initial team into Afghanistan to crucial contacts with the Northern Alliance before the American army could get their boots on the ground. His successor, Gary Berntsen, had played a critical role in the latter stages; particularly during the Battle of Tora Bora which targeted Osama bin Laden.

Colonel Sobhraj remembered the fallout from the operation's budget overrun. The bureaucrats had been livid, demanding detailed accounts and explanations. Yet, when the results were presented—the toppled regime, the captured operatives and the invaluable intelligence—the outcry had subsided. Success had a way of silencing critics.

Sobhraj took a deep breath, focusing back on the current situation.

"Sir," Lima said, "we also need a bike."

"A bike? Why?"

"All cable operators have one," Lima said. "We need to look the part. And it will also be our getaway vehicle once the job is done."

Lima's demands were high and the budget was strained, but Sobhraj knew that in the world of espionage, flexibility and quick decisions were paramount. Lima had proven his worth time and again. If he said they needed an additional fifty thousand takas, Sobhraj would find a way to provide it.

Colonel Sobhraj had someone from the accounts department transfer more money to his boys. Lima and Chad then went to a local garage to purchase a second-hand bike. There was a bike in good condition which would cost ten thousand takas more than what the duo had budget for. But given the constraints, they agreed to buy one which was not in such a good condition. The duo paid the garage owner and hopped on to the bike. They were halfway back to their rented room when the bike sputtered for a moment before regaining its momentum. Chad tapped Lima on the shoulder.

"What if the damn thing breaks down when we need it the most?" he said.

Lima shrugged and simply turned his wrist on the accelerator. Over the course of the next few days, Lima and Chad took over the business. The Agency also exported a bunch of Android set top boxes from China which they could demo to the existing customers and gain a pretext to get entry into their homes. With the set top boxes packed in Chad's bag, the duo would set out to find Akram's house.

The house-owners of course didn't recognise either Lima or Chad but they were more than willing to let the two inside their homes when told about the amazing functionalities of the new set top boxes. Lima and Chad knocked upon a door which was located at an intersection.

"Never saw you guys before," an old man who opened the door said. "And since when did our stingy cable operator begin caring to offer us new services?"

"We have entered into a contract with the cable operator dada," Chad said in Bengali. "From now on, we are in charge of the cable services for your area. Any problem, just call us."

Their demo was highly successful. People were liking the product and signing up. But when people wanted to install the box, Chad and Lima would say that the installation was due to start in a few weeks after sorting out some technical considerations. The man seemed impressed. Meanwhile, Lima, who was fiddling with the cable wires behind the TV set, cast one last sweeping glance across the living room before concluding that the house did not belong to the person they were looking for.

"We will put you on the waiting list," Lima said as he emerged from behind the TV set.

They walked out. But the same story played out again and again with different characters. Housewives. Husbands. Families. They had covered half the locality and still hadn't found a single sign of Akram's presence in any one of them.

"Where the hell is that bastard hiding?" Chad said. "Or was he already informed of our mission and went underground?"

"I don't think so," Lima said. "We have to keep looking."

The heat had drained both of them. Lima wanted to get to the room, hit the bed and sleep like there will be no tomorrow. The bike sputtered through the empty street to carry the two worn out Agency personnel to their rented apartment.

For dinner, the duo ate fish and rice and decided to sleep early. The two must have just drifted off to sleep when there was a knock on the door which brought Lima back to his senses and he quickly tapped on Chad's shoulder. Chad put his hand under the pillow and felt his pistol, whereas Lima put his weapon behind the small of his back and walked towards the door.

The rappings only got louder. Lima felt a hint of apprehension. After all, the sharp knocks on the door had come in the wake of one of their search trips looking for Akram in a cable operator's disguise. Lima trotted towards the door with wary steps.

"Who is it?" Lima asked once he reached the door.

No answer. With his guards raised high he slowly opened the door just enough to sneak a peek. He was straining his eyes to see through the narrow slit and identify the man standing at the stoop when a face suddenly appeared in front of him.

"Babumoshai!" said Rehman chacha, the landlord. "I got some sweets for you."

Lima forced a smile on his face and praised the landlord's efforts. "But this really wasn't needed, Uncle."

Rehman was in full mood to walk inside and chat with Lima and Chad. But Lima stood at the door, blocking his path so that he wouldn't have an easy entry.

"Where's your partner?" Rehman said.

Before Lima could answer, Chad made the loudest snoring noise he could. Lima moved just a bit, to give Rehman a full view of Chad's sleeping act. To complete the message to Uncle, Lima also yawned indicating his plans for the night. He could see the disappointment in Uncle's eyes. The man was really communication thirsty, a loner who put on a jovial act to convince himself that he was happy. But emotions meant little to Lima. He was a chameleon, after all.

***

Lima had begun sharing Chad's hopelessness when the next day's trip to another cluster of houses yielded no gains until later evening. He entered the next house with the air of a dejected soldier who was on the verge of a disappointing defeat. An old lady received them. While Chad played his part of introducing themselves as the new cable operators who had come to demo a new service and check the existing connection, Lima traipsed mechanically towards the TV set and started fiddling with the cable wires. His sombre mood did not allow him to spend much time feigning examining the wire and he stood up to leave after passing a few minutes trying to scan the house.

"Everything's fine here," Lima said, trying not to sound disappointed.

"Aunty-ji is also ready to sign up for the new set top box," Chad said. "Let me add her name and then we can get going."

Chad was writing the details down and asked for details of the houseowner.

"Mohammad Akram," the old woman said.

Chad and Lima looked at each other. "Is the owner at home?" Chad asked.

"He is out of the city, and will return in a few days," the old woman said.

Lima nodded. They had found a potential apartment for their suspect but would need confirmation if the man whom the old lady had mentioned was indeed their target; Mohammad Akram.

"Okay," Lima said to the old lady. He wrote his number on a piece of paper and handed it over to the lady. "Call me if there are any issues with the cable connection. We are at your service. Twenty-four hours, seven days a week."

The sudden upliftment in Lima's mood did not go unnoticed by Chad. He slightly nodded at Lima before asking for leave from the old lady. They came out of the house with a triumphant spirit. Later that night, Lima broke the news to Colonel Sobhraj who instructed Lima to make sure that Akram, if he was the one they'd come looking for, didn't get too suspicious.

"That wimp will slip away as soon as he learns that he is being surveilled," Colonel Sobhraj said.

Lima waited a few days to ensure the timing of his next act would be perfect. The narrow alley where the old woman lived seemed even more desolate under the dim light of dusk. Stray dogs barked in the distance. He moved swiftly following the cable line which snaked along the exterior wall of the house. *Snip.* With deft fingers, he disconnected it. He paused, listening for any signs of disturbance. A few minutes later, he received a call from the old woman.

"Our connection is not working," the old woman said.

"Be right there to fix it," Lima said.

In a few minutes, Lima reached the old woman's house and asked to check the cable connection. Of course, it wasn't working because Lima had himself disconnected the line. But it gave Lima a pretext to check if Akram was present in the house. It was late in the afternoon and Lima found that an Esteem car was parked outside the bungalow. He made a mental note of the registration number of the vehicle.

Inside the house, Lima looked for signs of Akram, but the man never came into his view. Lima went back to the place from where he had disconnected the line and got the connection working again. Then he called up the woman to inform that the line had been fixed. The woman checked her TV and confirmed that all was okay.

"Thank you very much," she said. "I didn't want to miss my favourite show in the evening."

Lima narrated the day's development to Chad, who believed that the appearance of the Esteem car indicated that the man who lived in the house was back in the city. The duo decided to keep an eye on the house for a few more days and see if they could get a visual on Akram.

A few days after his first attempt, Lima made another disconnection of the cable line so that he could again enter the suspect's house and see if Akram's identity could be confirmed. He was waiting after disconnecting the line when he got a call from the cable distributor from whom they'd taken over the dealership of the area.

"You better ensure services are running properly for my customers," the distributor said.

"Why?" Lima asked, his voice full of feigned innocence. "What happened?"

"I got a call from Akram saab's house," the cable operator said. "The man is furious that the line isn't working for the second time in a week."

"I'll be right there to get it fixed," Lima said.

From the cable operator's words, it seemed like the man was in the house and this appeared to be a golden opportunity for Lima to confirm his identity. Lima kicked the bike to a start and rushed to the suspect's home. Throughout the ride, he kept wondering if the man who had called the cable operator would turn out to be the same Mohammad Akram whose photograph had been passed to him in Colonel Sobhraj's office. No sooner than Lima had stepped into the bungalow, he faced the full fury of Akram's anger.

"Why the heck am I even paying you bastards each month?" Mohammad Akram screamed into Lima's face. "Every day my mother begins complaining about the broken connection."

"Sorry, sir," Agent Lima said. He was relieved that all their efforts had borne fruit and the coveted target was right in front of him. *Should I do it now? No. Not now.* For a spy like him, impatience was a deadly sin. Patience was a spy's greatest ally. It allowed for careful observation of crucial details that hasty actions would miss. Meticulous planning. Waiting provided the opportunity to strike at the most opportune moment. The art of espionage was as much about when to act as it was about how.

"Stop staring at my face," Akram said. "Fix the damn problem."

"Yes-sir," Lima said. He sure was going to fix *the problem* pretty soon. Resolving the connection issue which he had created, Lima returned to his rented room and confirmed the development to Chad, and later briefed Colonel Sobhraj as well. Since Akram and Lima had seen each other now, it was decided that Chad would conduct the relevant surveillance to identify Akram's travel routine.

Chad set up a post in the area, pretending to work with cable lines while keeping an eye on Akram's bungalow. Patterns began to emerge—the morning rituals, the guests who came and went, the times of the day when Akram's house resonated with life. Chad documented every detail in a small notebook and created a chronicle of Akram's existence. Meanwhile, Lima worked with Victor to set up a secondary safehouse where they'd retreat after the hit.

Chad mapped out Akram's travel routine with the meticulousness of a cartographer. He learnt that Akram would visit the local club each morning to play a few games of tennis. Armed with newfound knowledge, Chad retreated towards Lima.

"The dumbass can't even hold a racquet properly," Chad told Lima. "But wants to play tennis!"

"Let's take him out tomorrow," Lima said.

"On the way to the club?"

Lima nodded. "The crowd is thin early in the morning."

Chad agreed. He had studied the route already. There was a comparatively lonely stretch on the road which was ridden with potholes. Akram's car would slow down at this point. And then—bang, bang.

The stage was set. Pieces arranged. Chad was driving the bike and Lima was riding pillion. The Star pistol with an attached silencer lay safely tucked in the small of his back. Chad had worn a helmet whereas Lima had covered his face with a handkerchief, which was a common practice amongst the local populace as a safety measure against air pollution.

Chad maintained a safe distance between their bike and Akram's car. The car took the turn to hit the pothole-ridden stretch of road. Chad followed the car on the patch of the road and shifted gears. The distance between the car and the bike started minimising.

Lima slid his hand under the shirt and wrapped his hand around the clammy metallic butt of the pistol. He was all set to draw and pull the trigger when Akram spotted the bike coming dangerously close and veered his vehicle close to the left side of the road. This move did not grant Chad enough space to pass through and get the bike in the right position for Lima to take a shot at Akram with his right hand.

"Get to the other side," Lima told Chad.

Chad cruised the bike over to the other side of the car. Lima whipped out the pistol with his left hand. He looked through the tinted window and pulled the trigger thrice. Muffled sounds escaped the muzzle of the pistol. The next moment, Akram's head slammed against the steering wheel of the car. Cracks like spiderwebs appeared on the window.

The windshield was smeared in blood and the car cruised along a few paces before crashing into the wall ahead and stopping dead in its tracks. The impact caused the car's boot to come open. Chad stopped the bike while Lima hopped off the seat and scrambled to look into the contents of the trunk.

He was surprised to find out that Akram was carrying a cricket kit in the trunk of his car while on his way to the tennis court. Sensing something fishy, he decided to scour through the kit. Reaching the bottom of the bag, his eyes widened when his sight fell upon layers and layers of money.

"That's a lot of money," Chad said, easing his grip on the clutch so that the bike could speed off. "Who was he going to deliver it to?"

"Doesn't matter," Lima said. "The bastard had stolen the Agency's money. Let's consider this as repayment and get the hell out of here."

***

Lima and Chad reached their primary room carrying the bag filled with money. Chad slipped under the bed to pick up the bag that contained their mission equipment. Soon the news of Akram's dead body being discovered on the road spread all across the town and the ISI was quick to pile up the pressure on the local police. The police hastily gave a statement that Mohammad Akram was killed due to a highway robbery of the two crore takas that he was carrying in the boot of his car. Lima knew that they had to get rid of any suspicious belongings and decided that they would move the money and their equipment to a safehouse which Victor had arranged for them.

Perhaps, the Bangladeshi authorities knew very well that Akram had been targeted by Indian Agencies but refrained from making it public as Akram was also involved with the ISI. Lima stuffed the pistol into the bag, picked up their satellite phone and gestured to Chad to follow him out of the room. He locked the door and told Chad to drive the bike to a safehouse.

They reached the secondary room, more than fifty kilometres away and shifted the equipment there. Lima called Sobhraj using the satellite phone.

"Stay put for at least a week before we make arrangements for your return," Colonel Sobhraj said over the satellite phone. "Continue to stay in your primary room until then. Business as usual."

Lima wanted to inform the Colonel about the seized money but stopped short of knowing that the Colonel wouldn't have appreciated the fact that he spent time scouring through the boot of Akram's car.

Lima and Chad headed back to the primary room. The streets appeared eerily silent and unusually deserted. Each gust of air hitting his back was unsettling, as if it bore the ugly tidings of an ominous event. But Lima's instincts were warning him of something going awry. Late one night, Lima and Chad were about to sit down for dinner when Lima announced a sudden change of plan.

"Grab the keys to the bike," Lima said, pushing his plate aside.

"Are we eating outside?" Chad said. "All the hotels must be closed at this hour."

Lima was unusually impatient as he took the keys from the drawer and stomped out of the house. Chad followed his partner. This time, Lima was riding the bike and Chad was pillion. Chad soon figured out that they were headed for the secondary safehouse.

"Why are we going there?" Chad asked.

"I want to make sure our stuff is safe."

"What makes you think it's not?"

"That's what I want to find out."

As they approached the safehouse on the outskirts of the city, Lima turned off the headlights and slowed down the bike. He parked the vehicle a few hundred metres away and then the duo began making their way towards the house in stealth mode. Lima and Chad noticed that an unmarked vehicle was parked outside the gate of the house. Two men with crew cut hair were standing with their hands on the hood, and they were soon joined by three more men who emerged from the safehouse with two bags in their hands.

Lima recognised the bags as the ones which contained the weapons and the cash. He looked at Chad who was now taking Lima's concerns more seriously.

"We can't return to the primary room," Lima said.

Chad agreed. "They'll probably be raiding it right now."

"We'll have to go back," Lima said.

"Where?"

"Back to where we came from."

Lima started the bike and the duo began riding back towards the border village through which they had entered the country. The crisp night air whipped through Lima's hair as the motorbike hit the highway and roared towards the roads leading to the border. Chad, riding pillion, scanned the surroundings with a watchful eye. At times, Chad felt that every car that was approaching them belonged to the Dhaka Police or the BDR who were following them, and his anxiety would only ease after the vehicle would flash its headlights and overtake them. The night held its breath, as if the world itself was aware of their clandestine mission.

Chaos and uncertainty seemed hot on their trail. Lima's grip on the handlebars tightened as he navigated the winding path. His mind calculated every move. His gaze focused on the dark shadows that danced along the edges of the moonlit road. The border loomed ahead like an elusive destination. Lima and Chad took turns on the bike, stopping only a couple of times for snacks, fuel or relieving themselves. Otherwise, they rode non-stop for fifteen hours. The pillion rider would sleep with his head resting on the main rider's back. The plan was to dump the motorbike a few kilometres before reaching the village which they had crossed on their way inside. But they were about 12 kilometres away from the destination when the second hand bike, which had served them well until this point, sputtered to a stop. Lima shook his back to alert Chad, who woke with a start.

"Huh? What?" Chad said.

"The bike," Lima said. "It's dead, Chad."

"What? Let me try."

Chad tried his hand at starting the two-wheeler. The petrol tank was half full. He tried to clean the spark plug and also a push start when everything else failed. Nothing. Lima and Chad pushed the bike into a nearby ditch and covered it with foliage. Then the duo stopped a truck which was headed in the direction of the village and hitchhiked a ride. The truck dropped them on the bypass and then the duo walked their way towards the house of the Agency man who had sheltered them on their way in.

The man was aghast at seeing the unexpected guests. "I wasn't expecting you," he said.

"We had no choice," Lima said. "We have to go across."

"Come inside," the man said. "Quick."

There was not much discussion inside the house except that Lima asked the man to take them across the border in the cover of the night. Since it was late evening, the man advised that they'd head out in the cover of the darkness, late night.

"Until then," he said, "eat something and get some rest."

When night fell, the man led Lima and Chad back towards a point from which the duo was on their own. "Go straight," the man told them.

Cloaked in the darkness, Lima moved with the precision of a ghost, navigating the rugged terrain with calculated steps and silent determination. The mission demanded utmost stealth, and Lima, a master of evasion; a chameleon, blended seamlessly into the obscurity of the night. The dense foliage became an ally and camouflaged Lima as he manoeuvred through the wilderness. The agent's training and instincts worked in tandem, ensuring a seamless traversal of the treacherous terrain. The sound of rustling leaves and the soft murmur of the night breeze masked Lima's movements, allowing the agents to breach the border undetected. Finally, they were back in their own territory. *Home.*

***

Lima sat across from Colonel Sobhraj in the austere officer's cabin, the echoes of their mission still resonating in the walls around them. Reports and maps lay scattered on the desk between them. The silence between them was heavy, fraught with unspoken words and lingering tension. Lima finally broke the quiet, his voice carrying the fatigue and gravity of recent events.

"We got him, sir," Lima said. "Akram is no longer a threat."

Colonel Sobhraj nodded. "Good. Eliminating him was crucial. He had sensitive information about our assets that could have caused significant damage if leaked to the ISI."

Lima leaned forward. "He was the architect of the fake Indian currency flooding Kolkata. Each note was almost identical to the real one. The economic impact alone justified the mission. But it was more than that."

Sobhraj's eyes narrowed, urging him to continue.

"Gamma and Charlie," Lima said, his voice dropping. "They were executed because of him."

"Yes," Colonel Sobhraj said. "We had to act, not just for the Agency but for them. Their deaths demanded justice."

Sobhraj sighed, the heavy responsibility of command visible in the lines on his face. His mind reeled back to the time when the CIA had acted strongly after their agent, Kiki Camarena, was abducted and murdered in Mexico. The CIA and DEA unleashed hell on the Guadalajara Cartel by launching Operation Leyenda. They captured and brought to justice those responsible for Camarena's death. It was a relentless pursuit that showed no mercy. The Agency needed to show the ISI and anyone else watching that they wouldn't tolerate their operatives being targeted.

Colonel Sobhraj stood up, walking to the window. He stared into the distance, his silhouette rigid. "Akram's elimination serves multiple purposes. It disrupts their operations, but it also signals our resolve. The ISI will think twice before making another move against us."

Lima nodded, the fire in his eyes undiminished. "Understood, sir."

Colonel Sobhraj gave a curt nod, his authoritative presence reasserted. "Dismissed, Agent Lima. Get some rest. We'll need you at your best for what's to come."

As Lima exited the room, the enormity of their mission lingered in his mind. Yet, amidst the heavy burden of loss, a fierce resolve ignited within him. He was determined to honour his fallen comrades by turning their sacrifices into a stronger, more secure Agency. The night outside was biting cold. The conflict was far from over. But a significant victory had been claimed, and Agent Lima had avenged his fallen comrades.

***

The afternoon light filtered through the windows of the Asiatic Library, casting a warm glow over the rows of ancient books and manuscripts. Mr Zaidi leaned back in his chair, a contemplative look on his face. His eyes scanned the room filled with rows of bookshelves reaching up to the high ceilings.

"It's fascinating, Lucky," he said. "Covert operations of the Agency have not only protected our borders but also influenced the course of history in the subcontinent."

Lucky Bisht nodded, his expression resolute. "These aren't just intelligence games; they're battles that shape the core of our regional security."

"The story of Bangladesh's emergence and the ongoing shadow war in Dhaka highlights the delicate balance we maintain," Mr Zaidi said and stood up to leave.

As they exited the grand library, the hum of Mumbai's streets seemed a distant backdrop to the narratives they had explored. Traffic bustled on both sides of the road leading to the Asiatic Library. Each footfall echoed the sacrifices and triumphs of countless operatives whose tales were woven into the fabric of history. Mr Zaidi and Lucky Bisht parted ways with a firm handshake, a silent acknowledgment of the battles fought and those yet to come. The story of RAW's instrumental role in the formation of Bangladesh and the intricate espionage in Dhaka remained with them; a powerful reminder of the unending conflicts that sculpted the destinities of nations.

five

Chandel Conspiracy

The Bada Kabristan in Mumbai, a sprawling Muslim cemetery in the Marine Lines area of South Mumbai, was a solemn place where the whispers of the past mingled with the present. Established in the 18th century, it has served as the final resting place for many. It was bordered by Chandanwadi, a Hindu cemetery. For Mr Zaidi, the place served as a reminder that every man would be laid to rest one day or another. In the world of many differences, this fact was constant. The cemetery's historical significance was etched into every weathered stone and moss-covered pathway.

Mr Zaidi stood near a grave, his head bowed in quiet reflection, paying respects to someone who had passed long ago. He cupped his hands and prayed. When he finished and turned around, he found Lucky Bisht waiting for him at the gate.

"Many of my colleagues have laid down their lives in the line of duty," Lucky said. "In our line of work, success is often a ghost, unrecognised and uncelebrated."

"It's a thankless job," Mr Zaidi said.

"Our victories are buried deep in classified files, but our failures?" Lucky said. "They make headlines."

Mr Zaidi was well aware of this phenomenon across the world. The Bay of Pigs Invasion in 1961 was a failed CIA-led operation to overthrow Fidel Castro's regime in Cuba, ending in disaster with most of the exiles captured or killed. Then there was the Iran-Contra Affair in the 1980s, where covert arms sales to Iran were used to fund Nicaraguan rebels, leading to a major political scandal.

"But the true measure of an organisation," Lucky said, "is how it deals with failure. Can it rise, learn and strike back?"

Mr Zaidi's curiosity piqued. "You've seen it firsthand?"

Lucky sighed. "Yeah. Let me tell you something about Agent Lima. A mission went horribly wrong. He broke off all contact with the Agency, tried to disappear." He paused. "But in our world, you can't stay hidden from your own for long."

***

May 2015: Circa 2015, Agent Lima had broken off all contact with the Agency and was trying to adapt to the life of a civilian. A mission had gone horribly wrong, and though Lima had lived to tell the tale, he wasn't keen on working for the Agency anymore.

During this period, Lima spent most of his days alone in Uttarakhand. But even the state's rich cultural heritage and verdant forests couldn't ease the aftermath of his fallout with the organisation he had served. However, in these moments of feigned forgetfulness, the perceptions of the world weighed least on Lima's shoulders.

His solitude was often intruded by calls from Delhi. Emissaries of Colonel Sobhraj would contact him, letting him know that the senior officer of the Agency wanted to speak with him. Operatives from the Agency also found their way to Uttarakhand to seek out Lima with a persistence that bordered on desperation. One quiet afternoon, Lima was sitting in the verandah when he received such a call.

"Colonel saab wants to speak to you," the caller said.

"I am repeating for the fifth time," Lima told the caller. "I am not interested in talking to anybody."

Lima remained steadfast in his dismissal and turned away each envoy with part defiance but also part self-preservation. Lima's family was also relieved to see him again and would warn him against embarking on new adventures. His mother would become particularly worried if he went missing for more than a few hours without declaring his whereabouts.

But a part of Lima also yearned for the rush of adrenalin that he had become addicted to. Dangerous dances of espionage and allegiance beckoned him beyond the tranquil facade of his current existence. Still, Agent Lima chose to keep the illusion of peace. With these refusals to the Agency, Lima's status grew, as a figure who operated on his own terms, untethered by expectations of those who once commanded his loyalty.

Days later, Lima was returning home on his motorbike after running an errand. Under the cloak of the night, Lima's vehicle sliced through the hush of Uttarakhand's alleys. The moonlight cast an eerie glow on the deserted streets. Cold air carried the faint scent of pine from the nearby forests. Lima's mind was preoccupied with the mission that had gone wrong, replaying each detail as he rode. The engine hummed against his thigh.

Lima focused on the path ahead. He stepped on the brake when an SUV cut across his path. Armed men spilled onto the road like spectres emerging from the depths. He swerved sharply, tires screeching. The men advanced towards his position. This was no random encounter; they were here for *him*. Lima's first instinct was to go for his desi *katta*.

"Wait," one of the men said. "We don't want any trouble."

"What do you want then?" Lima said.

"Get into the car," they ordered.

Lima could recognise them from their crew cuts and boots. These men worked for the Agency. He did what he was told, getting into the front seat of the vehicle. The SUV began speeding towards an unknown destination. Dense forests of Haldwani's borderlands began their undisturbed reign. The road meandered. Every now and then, canopies parted to reveal glimpses of the starlit sky. Higher elevations offered brief vistas over deep valleys which remained shrouded in the mist, creating a landscape that seemed to belong to another world. The rhythm of the car's engine mixed with the occasional call of nocturnal creatures. Agent Lima could identify with such creatures, for he was also a creature of the night, one who worked best in the shadows of darkness.

The car finally stopped at a safehouse which was nestled on the edges of civilization. Lima was caught in the web of his past allegiances. The safehouse was an unassuming proof of secrecy. Its exterior was a blend of rustic charm and deliberate neglect. The building was designed to evade notice with weathered walls.

Accompanied by the men, Agent Lima stepped inside. The space transformed. Rooms were equipped with bare necessities. An array of surveillance equipment blinked silently in the dark. This place was a hub of clandestine activity where strategies were forged and fates were decided. And one such decision-maker—Colonel Sobhraj, the Phantom—was seated at a wooden table.

Sobhraj's posture stemmed from decades of military discipline and bore an imposing presence. His eyes sat beneath a furrowed brow like the tales of the battles he had fought in silence. His cropped salt-and-pepper hair added an air of seasoned authority to his stern visage. Agent Lima found himself face-to-face with the very person he had been avoiding.

"Subtlety wasn't going to bring you back," Colonel Sobhraj said.

"Why do you need me with so many men at your disposal, sir?" Lima said.

"Maybe I don't," Colonel Sobhraj said.

The simplicity of his statement coupled with the unwavering determination in his eyes underscored the gravity of the situation. He put down a piece of paper and a pen in front of Lima. "I only need the names and contacts of your sources in the northeast."

Lima looked the other way. *"Protect your sources."*

"I taught you that lesson," Colonel Sobhraj said.

"Absolutely, sir. I haven't forgotten it; yet."

"Listen, Lima." Colonel Sobhraj leaned forward. "I did whatever I could to save you during the botched operation." He paused. "But right now, I am trying to avert a *major* tragedy."

Colonel Sobhraj, a master of psychological tactics, knew that direct persuasion might not sway Lima. The man had grown wary of the Agency's intentions about him. Instead, Sobhraj opted for a more nuanced approach and aimed to ignite the dormant spark of patriotism he knew still flickered within Lima's heart.

"Your faith in the Agency has wavered," Sobhraj said. "But this is not about the Agency. This is about the country. Your country. And mine." He paused. "The threat out there jeopardises not just the integrity of our nation but the safety of its people. You don't want to work for us? Fine." Another strategic pause. "But don't abandon your country, your brothers-in-arms."

The room seemed to shrink around Lima as Sobhraj spoke of duty, sacrifice and the greater good. The walls echoed with the Colonel's words. It was a calculated gambit which played on Lima's deeply ingrained sense of service to the country which had driven him to join the Agency in the first place.

Colonel Sobhraj watched closely for any sign that his words had found their mark in a heart which had grown cold with disillusionment. An unspoken conversation flowed between him and Lima. A silent clash of wills. They were two warriors;

each carrying their convictions and histories. Lima's resistance progressively lessened under Sobhraj's unwavering gaze. Finally, with a curt nod, he conceded. And in that moment, Agent Lima returned to a world he had vowed to leave behind.

"Very well," Colonel Sobhraj said. "Let me tell you what happened in Assam a few days ago."

***

A few days ago, in Assam, Inspector Biren Sarma was gathering his belongings to go home after another long day at the police station. The day's business had dwindled to a murmur; and Sarma looked forward to the quiet comfort of his evening tea, a brief respite in his otherwise relentless schedule. Just as he slung his bag over his shoulder, a constable approached him. Sarma's expression hardened. He only desired to leave the burdens of his badge at the door for the day. But his instincts were telling him that something was about to change.

"Sir, a thief in our custody is insisting to speak with you," the constable said.

"Should I waste my time on a petty thief's ramblings?" Sarma said. "Can't you handle it?"

"He claims to have vital information, sir."

The words hung in the air like a reluctant tether pulling Sarma back from the threshold of a well-earned break. With a sigh that carried the weight of his responsibilities, Sarma's resolve softened. Sarma conceded by putting his bag down with a resigned thud. The word *vital* carried too many implications to ignore even if it came from a seemingly unreliable source. His steps, directed now back into the heart of the station, echoed an internal conflict—a constant balancing act between scepticism and the slim hope of uncovering a lead that mattered.

Sarma made his way to the holding cells. The corridor stretched ahead, its walls lined with peeling paint and flickering fluorescent lights. The hum of conversations and the clinking of metal bars created a symphony of the station's ceaseless vigilance. In his years of service, Sarma had learned that truth often lurked in the most unexpected places. He was prepared to hear out the thief but was completely unaware that this conversation was going to be so pivotal to the history of military conflict in India.

In the harsh glare of the interrogation room, Inspector Sarma and the petty thief sat across from each other. Sarma's demeanour mixed scepticism with a seasoned investigator's instinct for the truth. He eyed the thief with a piercing gaze that seemed to cut through the facade of nervousness which the latter had worn like a poorly fitted garment. Sarma's opening was less a greeting and more a stern warning, a single line that set the tone for their exchange.

"This better be worth my time," he stated flatly.

The thief tried to negotiate. "Can I expect some leniency for what I am about to tell you?"

"Let's hear it first," Sarma said. "And then we'll see."

The thief's narrative unfolded like a venture into unknown territories. He recounted the tale of two mysterious girls from a foreign country who had crossed Indian borders and finally reached Assam. They had been travelling in a cab, speaking mostly in Mandarin. They seemed to know multiple languages and sometimes spoke with contacts over the phone in English and sometimes in the local dialects. Fragments of their conversation were pieced together by the cab driver (who happened to be a friend of the thief).

"Seems like they were up to some mischief," the thief said. "And they were going to meet someone."

"Why?"

"For some suspicious activity, hushed in secrecy."

"Who were they going to meet?" Inspector Sarma asked.

"A powerful man, probably one from the many militant groups in the state."

The mention of a mission and a powerful contact sent ripples of concern through Sarma. It was a thread that could unravel plans with potentially grave implications for national security. With minimal words exchanged further, Sarma acknowledged the gravity of the information.

The thief's revelation had unexpectedly steered him into the murky waters of international intrigue where an overheard conversation could be a piece of a much larger puzzle.

There were numerous instances in India's history where seemingly vital information had been overlooked because it came from a source that didn't seem worthy enough to possess such intel in the first place. One example of this was the 1993 Mumbai Bomb Blast. The Mumbai Police had arrested a few suspects in petty cases who claimed that they had information that the Bombay Stock Exchange, Airport, Mantralaya, etc. were all going to be blown up with bombs. The cops laughed it off because the very idea seemed absurd. *Multiple bomb blasts in Mumbai? Pfft.* Indeed, it sounded laughable—until it actually happened.

When Sarma stumbled upon potential evidence of infiltration by Mandarin speaking women in the northeast, the protocol for dealing with such sensitive information was immediately activated. The information was swiftly relayed to the Intelligence Bureau (IB), India's premier internal intelligence agency and was subsequently passed to other agencies using the Multi-Agency Centre (MAC).

The MAC, nestled within the Intelligence Bureau's framework, was formed in the aftermath of the 2001 Parliament attack. The MAC fostered seamless intelligence sharing among varied national security entities in real time. It served as a 24/7 operations centre to bridge the gap between central intelligence agencies, state police and central police organisations through its extensive network which includes Subsidiary Multi-Agency Centres (SMACs) across states. This arrangement promotes the upward and downward flow of intelligence and also enhances the nation's ability to pre-empt and counteract terrorist activities efficiently.

From the MAC, the information about the two mysterious women cascaded through the network of Indian intelligence and security agencies. And that is how Colonel Sobhraj had found the memo on his table. He now had to investigate these two women. *What sinister intentions did they hold?*

The mention of infiltration into the northeast touched upon a nerve that has been raw for decades. The region had been a hotbed for insurgent activities with its strategic geographical position and diverse landscape of ethnicity. Inherent fault lines continued to be exploited by foreign powers seeking to destabilise India. The porous borders, especially those shared with Myanmar, facilitated illegal crossing of individuals and also the smuggling of arms and narcotics which fuelled insurgency in the northeast even further.

Assam shared a land border with China in the northernmost regions. The border extends approximately 500 kilometres through different terrains such as mountains and plains. Infiltration wasn't not an unknown phenomenon in the region. Among the mosaic of insurgent groups operating in the northeast, the United Liberation Front of Assam (ULFA) led by Paresh Barua and the National Socialist Council of Nagaland (NSCN) with factions led by S.S. Khaplang were particularly prominent.

ULFA was formed in 1979 amidst growing dissatisfaction with the Indian government's handling of local issues in Assam. Led by Paresh Barua, the group emerged with the objective of establishing an independent state which would be free from

Indian rule. ULFA capitalised on ethnic and economic grievances, employing guerrilla warfare tactics, bombings and kidnappings to further their cause. This insurgency marked a significant chapter in Assam's history by challenging the Indian state's authority and prompting extensive military responses.

NSCN, led by S.S. Khaplang, remained a prominent insurgent group in northeast India. Formed in 1980, it split from the original NSCN due to ideological differences. Khaplang's faction advocated for a sovereign Nagaland. Operating mainly along the India–Myanmar border, the group engaged in guerrilla warfare, targeting Indian security forces and rival factions.

Colonel Sobhraj was well aware that the two groups had waged prolonged campaigns against the Indian state while demanding sovereignty. Guerrilla warfare, kidnappings and bombings were signature marks of their operations. Significant challenges had been posed to India's efforts to maintain peace and order in the region by these groups. Their involvement in cross-border smuggling and their alleged connections with operatives from neighbouring nations have been a source of continuous concern for Indian security agencies.

The information about the two women, potentially operatives from across the border who were sent to meet insurgent leaders in India, was met with grave concern. Colonel Sobhraj understood the implications it could have on national security.

His response was swift; agents were deployed across the northeast, with a particular focus on Assam; to track down these women and uncover their mission. However, the task was made daunting by the northeast's rugged terrain and complex social fabric where multiple ethnicities and languages overlap. Despite the best efforts of Sobhraj's men, tangible leads were hard to come by. The women, if they were secret service operatives, indeed, had covered their tracks well.

Colonel Sobhraj, a veteran of many such operations, was not one to be deterred by initial setbacks. In the world of intelligence, patience was as vital as action. Absence of substantial leads did not mean the threat was non-existent; rather, it signified that the operation needed to adapt. He wanted an agent who had the best intelligence network in the northeast, one who could probe deeper into forests and the valleys and find the proverbial needle in the haystack. He needed: Agent Lima.

***

After a period of deliberation with Colonel Sobhraj, Lima had conceded to return to the fold. His decision was borne out of a complex mix of duty and patriotism. It was the end of his self-imposed exile. The next morning, Agent Lima set out from Uttarakhand, the state that had been his sanctuary to head towards his *karmabhoomi*, the northeast of India, where he'd spent a lot of time during his service.

Assam's undulating terrain and a history steeped in both beauty and bloodshed was waiting for him. The journey was long and arduous and took Lima from the familiar landscapes of Uttarakhand into the heart of the northeast. Winding roads cut through dense forests and misty valleys, each turn revealing glimpses of remote villages nestled in the hills. The air carried the state's complex socio-political fabric. But the lush landscapes could barely conceal the scars of conflict and the undercurrent of unrest.

Lima navigated the streets of Guwahati with a familiarity bred from years of operating in such environments. After checking into a hotel, he headed for a night market, a place that appeared merely as a local gathering spot but was known among a select few as a nexus for clandestine meetings. Lima was looking to meet SD, a source whose reliability and depth of local intelligence had proven invaluable in the past.

SD, or Surya Dev, was a man of few words but many connections. His network sprawled across the ethnic mosaic of the state. Lima was holding a local English newspaper in his hand. The front page was filled with news of India's Act East policy.

Emphasising external security measures, the Narendra Modi government had come to power in 2014 and implemented the Act East Policy, first announced in November 2014, over its precursor which was called Look East policy.

Act East Policy underscored a strategic approach to security and development in northeast India. As part of the policy, Coordinated Patrols (CORPAT) with neighbouring countries, particularly Myanmar, exemplified India's efforts to secure its borders against insurgency. Additionally, projects like the India–Myanmar–Thailand Trilateral Highway and the upgrading of surveillance and border security mechanisms were part of a broader strategy to improve connectivity.

China had exhibited concern over India's Act East Policy due to its strategic implications in the Asia-Pacific region, where the dragon sought to assert its own influence. India's efforts to bolster its strategic and military ties with countries that have competing territorial claims with China, such as Vietnam and the Philippines, added another layer of complexity to Sino-Indian relations. Strengthening of India's relations with the United States and Japan through formats like the Quadrilateral Security Dialogue (Quad) also raised concerns for China about the strategic encirclement.

Infrastructure and connectivity projects under the Act East Policy, which improve access and influence in the region, were seen by China as moves to counterbalance the Belt and Road Initiative (BRI). While the Act East Policy was not explicitly aimed at containing China, the strategic undertones of India's increasing presence and partnerships in China's periphery were closely monitored by Beijing. Lima was completely aware about all of this.

In the enveloping darkness, Lima arrived at the night market which buzzed with an energy that defied the late hour. He blended into the crowd and navigated through the labyrinth of stalls. Scents of local cuisines—smoky, spicy and sweet—mingled together. He had worked in the region long enough and his stomach was accustomed to the palette of the food.

The market was a cornucopia of wares. Handcrafted jewellery glittered under the makeshift lights. Colourful textiles hung like rainbows captured in cloth. Stalls were laden with local spices, their strong flavour promising to transform any dish into a culinary masterpiece. Amid these, electronic gadgets of dubious origin vied for attention.

Lima, however, walked to a particular stall that seemed out of place with its array of counterfeit sneakers laid out with a semblance of order. The sign proclaimed a misspelt name of a famous brand in bold letters. Designs beneath it were imitations, albeit convincing. He approached the two young boys in their teens who were manning the stall and inquired about a specific pair of sneakers—a model that was popular yet hard to find in these parts.

"I'm looking for a pair of sneakers," Lima said.

"Which ones?" one of the boys asked.

"Straight Drive," Lima said.

The boy's eyes narrowed for a moment. "Ah, those," he said, "We have them, but not here."

"Where, then?"

"At our godown," the boy said. "Follow me."

Lima followed the young boy as they left the other boy at the counter and began threading their way through narrower alleys. The farther they moved from the market, the more the sounds of commerce and chatter faded. Lima could hear the occasional bark of a stray dog. The boy led him to an old godown where the coveted *sneakers* awaited him.

Inside the godown, the scent of rubber and fabric was a far cry from the aromatic richness of the market Lima had left behind. The place was a cavern of boxes and merchandise, a hidden trove of goods where the lines between genuine and imitation were blurred. Lima was asked to wait in a small room. Moments later, a man entered the room. Lima's face lit up at the sight of his old friend SD aka Surya Dev. Straight Drive was his codename.

Once a militant of the ULFA, SD had navigated the treacherous path from insurgency to a semblance of peace. He had transitioned to working with SULFA, an acronym for Surrendered United Liberation Front of Assam. The organisation was formed as a result of the peace and surrender process initiated by the Indian government and the state government of Assam. It was composed of former members of ULFA who had begun working for the government; and against the ULFA.

Roots of SULFA could be traced back to the early '90s. Significant surrenders of militants were facilitated after major military operations against the ULFA and peace talks initiated by the government. SULFA was born out of the desire of former militants to return to normal life. Many of them, like SD, were disillusioned by the prolonged conflict. The Indian government offered surrender and rehabilitation schemes, promised economic incentives, vocational training and integration into society for those who laid down arms.

SULFA members got involved in various activities post their surrender. Some took up civilian lives, leveraging government-offered rehabilitation programs. Others became informants or collaborators with security forces, using their knowledge of insurgent groups and networks to aid in counter-insurgency efforts. SD belonged to the latter category.

The duo began their discussion, and Lima mentioned the arrival of the two foreign, female agents. SD's expression turned grave.

"Yes, the two women did arrive. They're stirring the waters."

"What more can you give me?" Lima said.

"Not much. I've been out of the game. But I know someone who can."

Lima raised an eyebrow. "Ruby?"

SD nodded. "She's got her ear to the ground."

"Where is she?"

"In Manipur," SD said. "Covering a football match."

Lima had worked with Ruby before. Her expertise and connections had proved invaluable in some of his missions in the northeast. Her network spanned the intricate ethnic and political landscape of Manipur and made her an unmatched asset in the intelligence community. SD's revelation confirmed the arrival of the two agents and deepened the mystery. This also set the stage for Lima's next move—a reunion with Ruby in Manipur, where answers awaited amidst latent tensions.

***

Lima boarded a rickety, overcrowded bus and found himself wedged between locals. The journey from Assam to Manipur wound through beautiful landscapes. He watched as the bus navigated narrow, treacherous roads that clung to the sides of steep hills. Patches of wildflowers occasionally dotted the roadside, offering brief splashes of colour against the backdrop of dense greenery. The bus was filled with the low chatter of passengers which carried an undercurrent of vigilance—a reminder of the delicate balance between peace and unrest in this part of the world.

He rested his head on the window and pondered over the clandestine nature of intelligence work. The flow of information, he mused, was akin to a complex web of unseen rivers of the geopolitical landscape. To gather and infer such information required not only a keen mind but also an understanding of the cues hidden within human interactions and digital footprints. That is why, he often found himself navigating obscure lands, blending into foreign cultures. Each journey was a silent foray into the unknown. Some took days. Some took hours. Agent Lima, however, remained a constant traveller.

Upon reaching Manipur, Lima made his way to a local stadium where a football match was in progress. The stadium was ringing with the chorus of applause and boos. People from all walks of life had gathered to watch the match. The game unfolded with raw energy. The players were local heroes in their own right. They displayed a mix of agility and strategy, their movements on the field mirroring the complex intersections of unity and rivalry that characterised their homeland.

But more than the match, Lima was interested in the journalist who was covering it. From the press box, a figure detached herself from the throng of journalists and photographers. Ruby, with her keen eyes, had spotted Lima almost instantly. A silent acknowledgment passed between them—of past lives marked by conflict and survival. She made her way to meet him, navigating through the throngs of cheering spectators.

Ruby, once a militant, now wielded her pen with the same fervour she had once reserved for more lethal methods. Her transition to a journalist had been facilitated by Lima through the Agency.

In the northeast, where allegiances shifted like the monsoon winds, Ruby had carved her niche. She was once a bright-eyed university student with dreams of changing the world through her words. Soon, she got involved with the militant movement and worked as a manager of their media wing. Her trajectory altered drastically when she was recruited by the Agency, an arm of the country's security apparatus. Her inherent understanding of the region's complex socio-political landscape and her fluid adaptability made her an ideal candidate.

Trained in the arts of espionage and intelligence gathering, Ruby was reborn as a journalist. Her new identity perfectly veneered her role as Lima's source. Embedded within the fabric of Manipur's daily life, she wielded her pen and notepad as deftly as any spy gadget, crafting stories that informed her covert reports. Ruby's dual existence was balanced on a razor's edge. Her articles mixed mundane local events and coded messages to her handlers.

Meanwhile, the football match entered extra time. Fans erupted in cheers over a near miss. Lima seized the momentary diversion to lean closer to Ruby. His voice, barely audible over the roar of the crowd, carried a sense of urgency.

"The two female agents." Lima's eyes scanned her face for any telltale sign of evasion. "What were they doing in Assam?"

Ruby nodded subtly, ensuring her response remained cloaked under the guise of casual interest in the match. "They weren't just passing through, of course," she said. "They met *someone*."

"Who?"

"Someone who's been off our radar for decades," Ruby said.

"Need a name," Lima said.

"Paresh Barua."

Lima was stunned. His eye flicked to Ruby's for a fleeting moment, a spark of concern flaring in the depths, hinting at the magnitude of the situation. Paresh Barua's name resonated through the annals of the northeast's history. He was instrumental in the formation of the ULFA. In the late 1970s, amid growing dissatisfaction with the central government's handling of local issues, Barua and his compatriots founded ULFA to champion the cause of Assam's sovereignty. He emerged as a pivotal figure in shaping the organisation's military and strategic vision.

Barua had set the tone for ULFA's operations. Under his command, ULFA launched a series of attacks on the Indian forces and drew attention to ULFA's demands on both national and international stages. His mastery over guerrilla warfare tactics made the group a significant concern for the Indian government, prompting widespread efforts to quash the rebellion.

Barua held a deep understanding of the geopolitical landscape. He adeptly navigated the complex network of international support and sanctuary, securing arms and training for his cadre.

Throughout the tumultuous years of ULFA's campaign, Barua remained an elusive figure—a ghost. He was believed to have moved out of India in the early 1990s to evade capture by Indian security forces. Then he worked to establish international connections that could support ULFA's insurgency. His ability to operate from abroad remained a crucial factor in sustaining the groups' activities over the years and allowed him to coordinate operations, secure funding and procure arms from a position of relative safety.

Lima's mind pieced together this new information with the fragments he already possessed.

"Our information says that he is not in India," Lima said.

"Then, my friend, you need new information," Ruby said. "I'd think that is what brought you here in the first place." She paused. "But you're late. Barua has already crossed the border."

"And the two girls?"

"They crossed over to Myanmar," Ruby said.

"What more can you give me?" Lima asked.

"I'm going to Myanmar next week," Ruby said. "I'll see what I can find out."

Ruby had a source in Myanmar, an officer of their army who had invited her to cover a football match for the local population. Lima was interested in knowing what more this visit would reveal. As usual, Ruby had retained the most important piece of information as her parting byte.

"Bisheshwar Singh's boys are expecting a few visitors."

"So the PLA is involved too?" Lima asked.

Ruby nodded. The People's Liberation Army (PLA) of Manipur, not to be confused with China's military force of the same name, was established on September 25, 1978, under the leadership of N. Bisheswar Singh. Formed with the aim of securing Manipur's independence from India, the PLA had been a significant actor in the insurgency in the northeastern region of India. Rooted in a deep-seated desire for sovereignty, the organisation has engaged in armed struggle against the Indian state for political autonomy.

"Where are these visitors arriving? And when?"

"The PLA area commander in Senapati district will know," Ruby said.

Senapati District was located in the northern part of Manipur. It was predominantly inhabited by tribes. The terrain, marked by hills and valleys, provides a strategic advantage, making it a vital area in the context of regional security and ethnic dynamics. The impact of militancy in Senapati District had been profound in its social, economic and political life. The region had its share of unrest with various militant groups operating within its boundaries leading to complex inter-ethnic and intra-ethnic dynamics.

Furthermore, security operations conducted by the Indian government to counter militancy also had significant implications for the local population. While aimed at restoring peace, these operations sometimes led to tensions between security forces and local communities. The interplay of militancy, ethnic identity and state response continued to shape the socio-political landscape of the Senapati District and made it a critical area in the discourse on peace and stability in northeast India.

Lima was aware of the implications now. The confirmation of the agents' presence in Assam—their clandestine meeting in Assam, and subsequent crossing to Manipur—suggested a convergence of interests that threatened to tip the already precarious balance of regional security.

***

The dense foliage of Senapati district was occasionally disrupted by the hum of vehicles. Agent Lima and his associates were stationed strategically along a deserted route. Their vehicle was parked inconspicuously off the road. Two of his team members patrolled the area on a bike.

Their target was the area commander of the PLA, who was known to frequent this path on his motorbike. Intelligence had pinpointed his schedule for the day and Lima's team was primed to act. The plan was simple; yet daring.

The sun began its descent. A distant rumble grew into the distinct sound of an approaching motorbike. The commander appeared and was riding with an air of unsuspecting confidence. Lima was ready. On his cue, the men on the bike accelerated, closing the distance before executing a precise manoeuvre that seemed like a loss of control. They crashed into the commander's bike, sending both parties skidding across the asphalt in a cloud of dust and debris.

Before the commander could fully grasp the situation, Lima and his associates were upon him. No sooner had they gotten close to him, Lima pulled out his weapon and aimed it at the commander.

"Get inside the bloody vehicle," Lima ordered.

Surrounded, the area commander did what he was told. The ride was swift. The commander's confusion grew with every turn that led him away from safety. Their destination was a secluded hideout, prepared in advance for such a moment. As soon as they reached the destination, the interrogation began. Bound and facing Lima across a dimly lit table, the commander put up a show of defiance. Yet, Lima's team worked on the man using a mix of psychological tactics and third degree methods.

"Tell us," Lima said. "When are your men crossing over?"

The interrogation went on for a while. Finally, the commander divulged that five men were planning to cross the Moreh border on the 1st of June. This piece of intelligence was first relayed to Colonel Sobhraj, who then arranged for increased vigilance across the said border. As the commander was secured for transfer to a more official holding facility, Lima and his team prepared for the next phase of their operation.

Nestled along the porous Indo-Myanmar border, the town of Moreh stood as a passage between two nations. However, its strategic location also made it a focal point for cross-border infiltration. Militant groups and illegal migrants often exploited the dense forests and hilly terrain to discreetly cross into India, evading detection by the security forces patrolling the area. These infiltrations not only posed a threat to national security but also complicated the socio-political dynamics of the region.

In response, the Indian government had ramped up surveillance and security measures in accordance with the Act East policy. It deployed advanced technology and increased the presence of border security forces to thwart these unauthorised entries. However, the rugged geography and the sheer expanse of the border made it a daunting task to completely seal off the route.

The vigil on the Moreh border reached its zenith on the day when the terrorists from the PLA were expected to cross over.

In the dense underbrush of the jungle, a special army team lay in absolute stillness. Their bodies melded into the environment and their camouflage gear rendered them nearly invisible against the forest floor. The special forces were primed for the imminent arrival of five operatives slated to infiltrate Indian territory under the cover of darkness.

Hours ticked by. Sporadic calls of birds could be heard in the distance. The soldiers communicated in silence. Years of training manifested into seamless execution of non-verbal cues and subtle gestures. But the wait just kept on getting longer. It appeared like the intel had betrayed their confidence, when a faint rustling broke the monotonous symphony of the jungle. *Their quarry was nearby.* The orders were also clear. The men were to be caught alive so that the larger sinister plans of the two female agents could be uncovered and thwarted.

Five silhouettes materialised. They moved, unaware of the trap that lay in wait. As they crossed the predetermined boundary, the ambush team revealed itself. The command to surrender boomed through loudspeakers, momentarily disorienting the infiltrators. Deeming themselves surrounded, the militants opened fire instead of surrendering.

A firefight erupted. The night was shattered by the piercing gunshots and shouts. The team's disciplined volley of fire was aimed to incapacitate, not to kill. It was important to capture the intruders for interrogation. Amidst the chaos, three of the operatives exploited the dense foliage to make their escape. The remaining two were caught in the trap set up by the team. They were quickly subdued and apprehended and transported to an army camp.

The captives later found themselves under the glaring scrutiny of harsh lights in the confines of an interrogation room. Across from them sat an interrogator whose presence commanded attention.

With years etched into the lines of his face, his demeanour was calm yet imposing. He had spent countless hours unravelling the minds of those who dared challenge the state. His approach was not of brute force but psychological finesse, peeling layers with each question. Even his pauses were filled with unspoken threats and promises. He was a master of his craft, understanding well that fear and hope were the keys to unlocking the most resistant of wills. The two captives had been pounded for hours before the interrogator had been sent in. *Softening the target*, they called it.

"The sooner you speak, the sooner your misery will end," he said.

One of the captives shifted uncomfortably, eyes darting towards his comrade, seeking an unsaid agreement. The interrogator noticed the silent exchanges.

"We know a lot about the organisation you work for," he said.

The captured operatives belonged to the PLA. Over the years, the PLA had conducted various operations ranging from guerrilla warfare to targeted attacks against Indian security forces. Its activities led to it being labelled a terrorist organisation by the Indian government, adding complexity to the ongoing conflict in the region.

"But we're more interested in the larger plan," the interrogator said.

"They have formed an umbrella."

"What *umbrella*?"

"We don't know much about the umbrella organisation, sir," the captive said. "But there is going to be an attack on the Indian forces like never before."

"Where? And when!"

"Only the people in Myanmar know about the time and location," one of the captives said. "But we know one thing…

the attack will be made on a unit that is moving in or out of the northeast."

The interrogator held his chin in his hands. This information would send shockwaves through the hierarchy. The notion of a consolidated enemy force necessitating a strategic reassessment of their approach to counter-insurgency operations. Questions abounded: What form would this impending attack take? Who were the masterminds behind this umbrella organisation, and what was their ultimate objective? As the captives had said, the answer to this question was buried in Myanmar.

***

Ruby's passage through the Moreh border was marked by strict security and meticulous procedure which mirrored the tension that had enveloped the region. High fences crowned with barbed wire flanked the dusty path leading to the border. Watchful guards, positioned at intervals, scanning the surroundings for any irregularities. She approached the immigration checkpoint.

The immigration office was nothing expensive. Officials in uniforms greeted Ruby. She presented her documents at the counter: a passport, well-worn from travel but meticulously kept along with other documents. After necessary checks, Ruby was allowed passage.

In Myanmar, an armed vehicle was already waiting for Ruby. Its heavy-duty frame suggested that it was designed for more than just transportation. Guards escorted her to the vehicle. Inside, air conditioning provided relief from the heat. The vehicle began its journey away from border areas. They travelled 45 kilometres through a landscape that gradually shifted from the sparse border town to fields and then to the organised chaos of a town preparing for a significant event—a football match that had the locals buzzing with excitement.

In this clandestine backdrop, Ruby began interacting with the organisers of the match. She learnt that the match was being conducted under the auspices of an umbrella organisation—a coalition formed by various factions of militant groups from the northeast of India and their supporters in Myanmar.

Such umbrella organisations were not uncommon in the world of crime and terrorism. Disparate groups with slightly differing ideologies or objectives often come together under a single banner for a common cause. Notable examples include the United Self-Defense Forces of Colombia (Autodefensas Unidas de Colombia, or AUC), a federation of right-wing paramilitary groups in Colombia, which fought against leftist guerrillas like the FARC and ELN as well as drug cartels. Another example was the Syrian Democratic Forces (SDF)—an alliance of Kurdish, Arab and Assyrian militias, primarily battling the ISIS and other extremist factions in Syria while also resisting the Assad regime.

As Ruby absorbed the charged atmosphere of the football match, her mind was preoccupied with the intelligence she had gathered about the factions of the umbrella organisation which had been named United Liberation Front of Western South Asia (UNLFW).

Representatives from many separatist groups were present at this match. ULFA had long sought the independence of the state from India, driven by a blend of ethnic pride and economic grievances. Despite crackdowns and peace talks, ULFA's core faction remained committed to its separatist agenda. Led by Paresh Barua, whom the two Chinese agents had met, the group had created much havoc in the northeast.

NSCN K (National Socialist Council of Nagaland–Khaplang) was a key player in the Naga insurgency and advocated for a sovereign Naga state. Split from the original NSCN in 1988, the Khaplang faction has engaged in fierce battles against Indian forces and rival Naga factions. Operating across the India–Myanmar border, its strategic positioning allows for cross-border insurgencies, complicating efforts to quell its activities.

KYKL, a Meitei nationalist organisation, operated primarily in Manipur. It demanded an independent state for the Meitei ethnic group. KYKL's manifesto remained steeped in cultural revivalism, seeking to eradicate what they perceive as corrupting influences on Meitei society. Their operations, often violent, targeted state forces and symbols of alleged cultural degradation.

PREPAK (People's Revolutionary Party of Kangleipak) was another insurgent group from Manipur. It fought for an independent Manipuri state since its formation in the late 1970s. Its activities were characterised by bombings, ambushes and strikes intended to weaken the Indian state's grip on the region. PREPAK's vision extends beyond mere separatism, advocating for a socialist framework in its envisioned state.

Within this complex web of militancy, Ruby's source hinted at a coordinated effort that was brewing an operation of *unprecedented* scale. These factions had found common ground in their resistance against the Indian state. The significance of their unity could not be underestimated, Ruby realised. The implications were clear: they were on the cusp of executing something destructively monumental, a statement that could redefine the conflict dynamics in the northeast.

As Ruby crossed back into India, her mind was a whirlwind of information and covert conversations. She rendezvoused with Lima at a secluded cafe. She spoke of the main factions in the umbrella organisation—ULFA, NSCN K, KYKL and PREPAK—each with its storied history of conflict against the Indian state. She detailed how these groups, once rivals, had now forged an alliance with a singular, ominous purpose.

Lima listened intently, the seriousness of the situation

getting deeper with every word. The conversation took a more sombre turn as Ruby mentioned that these groups were planning to execute something significant. The details were murky, the plans closely guarded but the intent was clear—a declaration of war.

Agent Lima relayed whatever he had learnt to the higher ups. The entire intelligence apparatus was trying to figure out what operation was being planned. But it was like finding a needle in a haystack. Lima was also left pondering about the "big mission" these groups aimed to execute. What were they going to do? A few days later, the answer would reveal itself in a ghastly manner.

***

In the morning hours of June 4, 2015, a military convoy comprising four vehicles, was en route to Imphal. The soldiers belonged to the 6 Dogra infantry regiment and were being moved from the Moltuk valley.

The Moltuk Valley is located in Manipur, India, near the border with Myanmar. The region is known for its rugged terrain, dense forests and strategic significance due to its proximity to the international border. Manipur is divided into two main geographical areas: the valley region, which is surrounded by hills and is home to majority of the population, and the hill regions that cover a significant portion of the state's area. The valley, nestled among these hills, is part of this complex geopolitical zone.

The armed personnel inside the vehicles shared quiet conversations which were bolstered by the camaraderie that only those who have faced adversity together could understand. Their eyes occasionally scanned the dense foliage that flanked the narrow road. The impending catastrophe lurking in those jungles was yet to show its ugly face.

The convoy wound its way through a corridor in the Chandel district. The air was humid and carried the sounds of distant wildlife and the rustle of leaves. It was a vivid reminder of the untamed wilderness that surrounded them from all sides.

Between the villages of Paralong and Charong, the serene silence was shattered by the deafening roar of gunfire. Insurgents, their faces obscured by the mist, launched a meticulously planned ambush on the convoy of the Indian Army. Explosive devices, planted with precision, detonated to create a symphony of destruction. The lead and rear vehicles of the convoy halted to a stop. Chaos ensued. The soldiers were highly trained for combat but caught off guard. They rushed for cover and returned fire towards the indistinct shapes of their assailants.

The insurgents leveraged their familiarity with the terrain and manoeuvred with lethal efficiency. They unleashed a barrage of gunfire and grenades. In the aftermath, the smouldering vehicles and the fallen soldiers amidst the debris of what was meant to be a routine transfer painted a harrowing picture of loss and defiance.

This brazen attack ultimately left twenty Indian soldiers dead and several wounded. This was not just a military assault; it was a calculated provocation. The shockwaves of this attack would reverberate far beyond the dense jungles of Manipur. The militants had sent a message inked in blood to challenge the authority of the Indian state. The Chandel ambush was a pivotal moment which went on to galvanise the Indian government and its armed forces into a resolve for retribution and set the stage for an unprecedented response. And though Agent Lima was licking his wounds, he was about to get thrown into the deep end of troubled waters again.

***

Mr Zaidi and Lucky stood near the gate. The cemetery, with its ancient gravestones and silent pathways, seemed a world apart from the chaos beyond its walls. Bada Kabrastan's old iron gate creaked in the evening breeze, a reminder of the history it guarded. Lanterns flickered to life along the path, casting a gentle glow that softened the starkness of the tombs.

"The Chandel Conspiracy nearly broke Agent Lima," Lucky said. "But that's the nature of our work. When we fall, we fall hard."

"And Agent Lima kept going?" Mr Zaidi said.

"Indeed," Lucky said. "His journey wasn't just about redemption. It was about the pursuit of justice."

The call to prayer echoed from a nearby mosque, blending with the distant sounds of the city. The two men stood there for a moment longer, absorbing the gravity of their discussion. Leaving the quiet of the Bada Kabrastan behind, Lucky proceeded to speak about the Indian establishment's response to the Chandel Conspiracy—and it was one like never before.

six

Operation Hot Pursuit

After hearing the story of the Chandel Ambush, Mr Zaidi offered to drop Lucky back to his home in Versova. The duo settled into a car which began crawling through the Mumbai traffic. Mr Zaidi navigated the streets of Mumbai with ease, weaving through the crowded streets as if it were a choreographed dance. Lucky Bisht reclined in the passenger seat, his eyes half-closed, watching Mr Zaidi's hands deftly switch gears and guide the car through narrow gaps between buses and auto-rickshaws, leaving mere inches to spare. Their conversation turned to the topics that both men often pondered.

Mr Zaidi spoke about Operation Neptune Spear, the covert mission carried out by the U.S. Navy SEALs on May 2, 2011, which resulted in the death of Osama bin Laden in Abbottabad, Pakistan. The operation, executed with precision and stealth, marked a significant victory in the global fight against terrorism.

"Have you ever thought about the role that Dr Shakil Afridi played in that mission?" Me Zaidi asked. "Afridi was a doctor in Pakistan who ran a fake vaccination campaign for the CIA. His goal was to gather DNA from the children in the Abbottabad compound, where Osama bin Laden was suspected to be hiding. It was a perilous operation, filled with deception and danger."

Lucky interjected, "Afridi's intelligence was crucial. It confirmed Bin Laden's presence in the compound. Despite the risks, he provided the final piece of the puzzle that led to one of the most significant operations in recent history."

"The American forces showed remarkable skill and coordination," Mr Zaidi said. "Conducting an operation behind enemy lines, with such precision, was truly commendable."

"In the aftermath of the Chandel ambush, the Indian forces launched an operation of their own," Lucky said. "A perfect blend of precise intelligence and lethal force."

"Tell me more."

"This mission was called Operation Hot Pursuit. Here's how it unfolded..."

***

In the wake of the 2015 Chandel ambush, activity around South Block in New Delhi began to reach critical mass. Architecturally, the South Block is a magnificent structure designed by the British architect Herbert Baker in the Indo-Saracenic Revival style and its construction was completed in the early 20th century. It houses the key offices of the Government of India and is a part of the grand Secretariat Building which is located at the corner of Rajpath and Rashtrapati Bhawan, facing the grand vista of the India Gate.

The South Block is host to the Prime Minister's Office (PMO), the Ministry of Defence (MoD), the Ministry of External Affairs (MEA) and the National Security Council (NSC). Due to the critical nature of the offices it contains, strategies regarding national security, international relations and defence policies are formulated and executed here. It is regarded as the apex power corridor of India where most important decisions are made.

The Chandel ambush was one of the deadliest attacks against the Indian Army in decades. It had left the nation in mourning and also raised a sharp challenge for the Indian government's stance on cross-border terrorism and insurgency.

Prime Minister Narendra Modi had come to power promising an assertive approach to national security. This event, hardly a year into his first term, had brought push to shove. It was time to walk the talk. On the day of the attack, the PM had tweeted: *Today's mindless attack in Manipur is very distressing. I bow to each and every soldier who has sacrificed his life for the Nation.*

At the helm of the defence establishment was Manohar Parrikar, then defence minister. Born on December 13, 1955, in Goa, Parrikar was a distinguished alumnus of the Indian Institute of Technology Bombay (IIT Bombay) where he completed his degree in metallurgical engineering. This background contributed to his reputation as a pragmatic and efficient administrator. One of the first meetings he attended was also marked by the presence of Home Minister Rajnath Singh and the Chief of Army Staff General Dalbir Singh Suhag.

Having risen through the ranks with extensive experience in counter-insurgency operations, General Suhag's demeanour was one of controlled aggression. The forces were put on high alert and every lead was being pursued to hunt down the culprits. A combing operation had already begun but it appeared as if the attackers had escaped to a point where they were safe; *or so they thought.*

The National Security Advisor (NSA), Ajit Doval, a veteran intelligence officer with a deep understanding of counter-terrorism operations was notably strategic in his initial public reaction. While maintaining a low profile in the media, Doval's response was action-oriented, focusing on gathering intelligence, coordinating with neighbouring countries and formulating a nuanced counter-insurgency strategy.

Initial reactions from India's political and military leadership painted a picture of a nation united in its response to the Chandel ambush. Public statements were calibrated to convey resolve and the promise of retribution. But behind the closed doors of the South Block and the Army Headquarters, plans were being laid out for a response that would not only seek to avenge the fallen but also aim to deter future acts of insurgency. The decision was to find out the location of militant camps across the Myanmar border—and destroy them with a vengeance.

As the nation rallied behind its leaders, the groundwork for what would become known as one of the most decisive cross-border operations in recent history was being prepared. The political, military and strategic contours of the response were being drawn to address the immediate aftermath of the ambush and set a precedent for how India would handle asymmetric warfare and cross-border terrorism in the future. In these high-level meetings, it was decided that the Special Forces, Parachute Regiment (Para SF) would lead the mission to break the spine of the militant organisations who had conducted the dastardly attack on the Dogra regiment.

The selection of the Para (Special Forces) for the mission to retaliate against the 2015 Chandel ambush was rooted in a combination of strategic necessity and the unit's legacy of excellence in special operations. Known for their rigorous training, versatility in unconventional warfare and daredevilry, the Para SF was the natural choice for this mission.

The Para SF, an elite component of the Indian Army's Parachute Regiment, traces its origins to the early days of World War II. Initially formed in 1941 as the 50th Parachute Brigade, it included the 151st British, 152nd Indian and 153rd Gurkha Parachute Battalions. This unit was part of the airborne forces that played pivotal roles in various theatres of the war, gaining valuable experience in airborne assaults and special operations.

The operational history of the Para SF includes successful engagements in a variety of contexts, such as the 1971 Indo-Pak war, the Kargil conflict in 1999 and numerous counter-insurgency operations across Jammu & Kashmir and the northeastern states of India. The primary element of the Para SF insignia is the Balidaan Badge which is worn exclusively by Para SF operatives. "Balidaan" translates to "sacrifice" in English and is a core principle of the Para SF ethos. The badge features a commando dagger pointed downwards, with wings extending upwards from the blade. The dagger represents the stealth, precision, and lethal capabilities of the unit, while the wings symbolise the airborne capabilities of the Para SF soldiers. At the base of the dagger is an open parachute, further emphasising their airborne insertion skills.

Their expertise in guerrilla tactics, reconnaissance and direct-action missions made them the ideal force to carry out precise strikes against the insurgent camps believed to be responsible for the ambush. But specific intel was needed for the special forces to act, and the responsibility of gathering this intel fell upon Colonel Sobhraj's team. And he had already despatched Agent Lima and other intelligence operatives to Myanmar to find out the location of the camps where the militants had taken refuge after the attack.

***

Twilight draped a murky veil over the dense forests of the Naga Hills, near the Indo-Myanmar border. The border stretched for 1,643 kilometres, marking the international boundary from the trijunction with China in the north down to the junction with

Bangladesh in the south. The forests were home to rich flora and fauna, with towering teak, mahogany and bamboo groves creating a dense canopy overhead which barely allowed the last remnants of daylight to touch the forest floor.

Agent Lima had been dropped at the edge of the forests by one of his team members in a vehicle. After that, he was on his own to cross the border and reach Myanmar. His mission was clear: to find out the location of the terror camps where the militants who had conducted the Chandel attack were hiding.

Now he was surrounded by a complex undergrowth of ferns, orchid and a myriad of medicinal plants known only to the indigenous tribes and the local wildlife that have adapted to life in these thickets. Rivers and streams, fed by the monsoon rains, weaved through this landscape.

As Agent Lima navigated this complex ecosystem, he was acutely aware of the terrain's challenges and secrets. The dense foliage provided both cover and obstacles. This area, straddling the invisible line between two nations, had been a silent witness to history's whispers. It had been home to ancient trade routes and contemporary conflicts.

Historically, India and Burma (later known as Myanmar) had operated a Free Movement Regime (FMR) for the tribal communities living along their common border, recognizing that the communities have age-old economic and cultural ties. The Burma Passport Rules of 1948 allowed indigenous populations of all the countries bordering Burma to travel to Burma without passports or permits, provided they lived within 40 km from the border. In 1950, India also amended its passport rules to allow the tribes people residing within 40 km around the border to travel to India and stay up to 72 hours.

In 1968, following a variety of insurgencies in its northeastern states, India unilaterally introduced a permit system for travelling across the border. This provision remained in place for the next forty years. In 2004, following the growth of drug trafficking and arms smuggling, India reduced the travel limit to 16 km and allowed border crossing only through three designated points: Pangsau (Arunachal Pradesh), Moreh (Manipur) and Zokhawthar (Mizoram).

Travel privileges aside, Lima navigated the treacherous terrain. His movements barely disturbed the dense underbrush. His knowledge of the land, honed through rigorous training and previous missions, guided him through the most obscure paths, minimising his exposure. He was in hostile territory.

A sudden rustle, a shift in the wind shot Lima's senses through the roof, and brought him to an absolute halt. The silhouette of a patrol became discernible through the dim light. They were moving at a casual yet vigilant pace that suggested familiarity and complacency with their surroundings. This was their domain and Lima's presence was an unwelcome anomaly that could not be discovered.

Lima turned into a statue. His body melded with the earth as if a part of it. He held his breath. They were close. He could hear the crackle of their radios. He felt like the last soldier on a battlefield against an enemy who had outnumbered him. But he relied on his training and skills to keep his breath and the beating of his heart under control, and waited in perfect silence for the patrol to pass.

As the patrol's footsteps faded into the distance, Lima emerged from his concealment like a wraith. This encounter was a reminder of the razor-thin margin between success and catastrophic failure. With renewed caution, he pressed on and disappeared into the darkness which was not just a cover now but a companion. He continued until he was deep into Myanmar.

Dawn broke over a remote village in Myanmar. The first rays of sunlight fell upon the thatched roofs and mud walls of the simple homes. This village, nestled in the grip of militant control, woke to another day of subdued existence. Residents here moved with the weary resignation of those long accustomed to living under the gaze of tyranny.

Agent Lima had arrived in the village under the cover of predawn darkness and blended into the local environment. After crossing the border, he had made his way into the house of an Agency contact who had helped him with clothes that would help him keep his disguise. Lima now wore a traditional longyi, a fabric wrapped around the waist, extending to the feet. He had paired it with a simple, worn-out shirt. His feet were clad in sandals, the kind favoured by locals for navigating the rugged terrain and muddy paths. A local hat, low over his brow and a weathered shoulder bag completed his guise. He looked like one of the village men heading out to begin their day's labour.

Lima was headed for an informant's house which stood at the village's edge, a derelict structure that leaned slightly to one side as if trying to withdraw from the world. Its bamboo walls were weathered by the elements. The roof's thatch was patchy from years without repair. A few kilometres away from the house was the farm where the villager now worked on his own.

The informant himself was a man whose life had been irrevocably altered by the conflict that enveloped the region. Once a farmer, he had been coerced into the militants' ranks during a time of desperation. Disillusioned by the brutality he witnessed and pained by the suffering of his community, he had eventually sought a path of redemption by becoming an ally to those opposing the militants. His appearance bore the marks of his turbulent past—a lean frame, hardened by physical toil and the burden of his secrets; his face, weathered beyond his years. Deep lines were etched into his forehead by constant worry and sleepless nights.

Lima approached the farm with the casual demeanour of a villager out for a morning walk. He scanned the surroundings with practised caution. He had ostensibly chosen the least conspicuous time in a village where every unfamiliar face could spell danger. The duo began chatting under the shade of a tree. Lima told the informant about the purpose of his trip. He wanted to know the location of the militant camps.

"This is dangerous. What if they find out?" the informant whispered, a tremor of fear lacing his voice. "Not just for me... my family."

"We can arrange safe passage, shelter for your family in another country," Lima said.

The informant thought about Lima's offer. Could he place his and his family's fate in the hands of someone like Lima, who navigated the murky waters of espionage where alliances were as brittle as glass? Doubt gnawed at him. A man who, in another life, might have been called a snake was offering him a better life. Here, he was caught in a perennial conflict and wanted a way out. He found himself pondering a gambler's chance. The stakes were invariably high.

"I'll lead you, but you must guarantee *our* safety."

Lima's reply was firm, a reflection of the unwavering commitment required in their line of work. "Once you've led us to the camps, I'll ensure your family's protection. But I need concrete evidence first. Without it, there are no guarantees."

The informant nodded. "Meet me tonight."

***

While Agent Lima was working in Myanmar, a strategic shift was on the horizon in India. Seventy elite troops from the Para Special Forces (SF) were being readied for rapid deployment to Manipur.

However, this operation was teetering on the edge of a knife, threatened by an invisible yet pervasive danger: the sophisticated network of support being provided to terrorist factions by their sympathisers.

History is replete with examples of high intensity guerilla wars being fought against professional armies. During the Vietnam War (1955–1975), the Viet Cong, a communist-led guerrilla force in South Vietnam, was notably supported by the local population especially in rural areas. This support was instrumental in their ability to conduct a protracted guerrilla war against South Vietnamese and American forces. The use of intricate tunnel systems built and maintained with the help of local villagers allowed the Viet Cong to launch surprise attacks and then disappear seamlessly into the countryside.

During the Soviet Invasion of Afghanistan (1979–1989), the Mujahideen fighters waged a successful guerrilla war against the Soviet Union with substantial local support. The terrain of Afghanistan and the local population's support, combined with foreign aid, allowed the Mujahideen to employ hit-and-run tactics effectively, eventually leading to the withdrawal of Soviet forces.

However, the key difference when compared to the Manipur situation was that the armies of other countries had invaded Vietnam and Afghanistan. In the northeast, the Indian Army was operating within its own territory to prevent any secessionist movement. However, it could not be argued that militant factions had a strong local information network.

These informants were not the cloak-and-dagger spies of novels. They could be anyone—from the disillusioned farmer, weary of the endless cycle of violence or the underpaid labourer looking to supplement his income. Others might include local sympathisers with deep-seated grievances against the state. These informants, embedded within the very fabric of daily life, had their ears to the ground. They were vigilant for any whispers of military movements, ready to relay this information back to their terrorist handlers. This web of eyes and ears had become a formidable barrier to operations against insurgent elements, threatening to unravel even the most meticulously planned operations.

Informants of militants had also developed a series of secret signals and codes to communicate information about troop movements. This could include the way clothes were hung to dry, patterns of rice planting or even the placement of everyday objects outside homes. These signals were seemingly innocuous to the untrained eye but conveyed specific information to the terrorists.

The revelation that the Para SF was mobilising for Manipur could lead to catastrophic outcomes. Forewarned, the insurgents could either vanish into the dense jungles, leaving the troops chasing thin air. Worse, they could prepare a lethal ambush designed to decimate the advancing Indian soldiers.

India's best military minds, including NSA Ajit Doval and COAS Dalbir Singh Suhag, discussed the issue at hand. Promoted to the rank of Lieutenant General, Bipin Rawat had been appointed as General Officer Commanding III Corps, headquartered in Dimapur. They decided that the Para SF would be moved to Manipur wearing the uniforms of the Bihar Regiment!

The Bihar Regiment, a storied infantry regiment of the Indian Army is known for its valour and distinguished service history. With battle honours spanning from the harsh terrains of Kargil to the jungles of the northeast, the regiment was a common sight in Manipur. Their presence was unlikely to raise any alarm. This ingenious strategy was a simple but powerful idea of military deception. It played on the enemy's overreliance on their informant network. The troops, camouflaged in the identity of the Bihar Regiment, moved towards Manipur.

After reaching Imphal, the team began the last leg of their

preparation before embarking on the mission. Valuable intel had been collected by Agent Lima about the target area, enemy forces, terrain and weather conditions.

Before embarking on an assault mission, a military unit undergoes extensive preparations, meticulously planning and coordinating every aspect of the operation to ensure the highest chances of success. These preparations are vital for the safety of the personnel involved and the achievement of the mission's objectives. Seventy elite soldiers, their features etched with resolve and the scars of countless battles, stood in an impromptu semicircle.

At the front, standing with authoritative ease before a makeshift table strewn with maps and satellite imagery, was the team leader, Major Arjun Singh. His presence was commanding, the kind of innate leadership that spoke of experience and commitment to the mission. His eyes, sharp and focused, scanned the room, making contact with his operatives. Working with his seniors, he had developed a detailed mission plan that outlined objectives, routes, timelines and contingencies.

"Listen up," Major Singh's voice cut through the silence, firm and devoid of any doubt. "Operation Hot Pursuit is about to commence. We are going deep into enemy territory. Our target is a high-value insurgent camp, nestled in the heart of the jungle, coordinates already briefed."

This was going to be a stealth operation. Speed, silence, and precision were going to be their allies. The Para SF was determined to strike hard and fast, neutralise the target and return to Indian territory. Major Singh walked to the map, his finger tracing the route of their insertion, the path winding through treacherous terrain.

"The insurgents are cunning, but we have the element of surprise. Intelligence confirms they're unaware of our move." He turned, facing his team directly, his gaze unwavering. "You were chosen for this operation because you are the best of the best. Your training, your instincts, and your courage will see us through."

The air was still, the only sound the soft rustle of maps as Major Singh rolled them up, a symbolic gesture marking the end of the briefing and the beginning of their mission.

The team dispersed to ready themselves, their minds and bodies honed instruments of war. Major Singh watched his team with a fierce pride in his heart. They were ready; so was he. The operation would begin soon. Next, the team began selecting and preparing the necessary weapons, ammunition and specialised equipment tailored to the mission requirements. It was necessary to ensure all gear was in optimal condition, including personal protective equipment, communication devices and navigation tools. There could have hardly been any question on the physical and mental conditioning of the team. The soldiers were amongst the best in the country.

Strict Operational Security (OPSEC) measures had already been put in place to prevent any information leakage about the mission. Phones and communication devices of the operatives had been secured. Major Singh reviewed the logistics support, including transportation, medical support and emergency extraction plans.

With all the planning conducted with military precision, it was time to leave. The rules of engagement were clear. *Take no prisoners.*

***

Back in Myanmar, Agent Lima met his informant at the predetermined rendezvous point near the thick foliage that marked the beginning of their treacherous journey. The informant's eyes flickered with a tumult of emotions. His feet wavered under imminent danger. His stance was tense. His body was manifesting the internal battle raging within him. Lima observed the informant's hesitation, understanding the fear and doubt that gnawed at the man's courage. He stepped closer, his voice low but steady.

"I know what's at stake here." Lima locked eyes with the informant. "But remember why you chose this path. This is for your family's future. For a life far removed from the perils of war."

The informant's gaze faltered. His mind wrestled with the gravity of Lima's words. He knew Lima was right; this was a chance to break free from the chains of his past. After a moment that stretched into eternity—he nodded.

They set off into the heart of the jungle. The path before them was fraught with peril. They traversed a landscape where every step on the moss-covered ground threatened to betray their presence with a misplaced footfall. Vines hung like serpents from the trees. The air was thick with the hum of unseen creatures, a constant reminder of the wild's indomitable presence.

The route they had chosen was known only to a few, a narrow trail that snaked through the dense undergrowth. Lima skirted around hidden ravines that yawned open like the mouths of giants. At times, the path climbed steeply. Lima used the gnarled roots that protruded from the earth as handholds, pulling himself up inch by gruelling inch. The physical toll of the trek, coupled with the psychological burden of what lay ahead, became a crucible too harsh for the informant. He halted, his breath heaving. Sweat mingled with the dirt on his brow.

"I can't," he gasped, his fear finally finding a voice. "I can't go any further."

Lima turned, his expression unreadable. "You've already done the impossible," he said and gestured towards the path ahead. "You can turn back now."

The informant looked into Lima's eyes. He found not just a

commander but a comrade, someone who shared the burden of the path they walked. With a deep, steadying breath, he found a reservoir of strength. From that point, Lima continued his journey into the heart of darkness and finally managed to find a vantage point.

Agent Lima's gaze first settled on the two militant camps through the lens of his night vision goggles. A cold, calculating calm settled over him. The sight of the enemy strongholds, stark against the night, transformed abstract intelligence into a palpable reality.

Lima initiated a critical phase of the mission: the overnight reconnaissance of the militant camp. The camp, a hub of hostile activity, lay sprawled in a clearing a kilometre ahead. Given the need for silence and stealth, drones and other remotely operated devices were out of the question. Instead, Lima relied on a suite of high-tech yet realistically deployable, surveillance equipment.

The primary tool in Lima's arsenal was a set of Gen IV Night Vision Goggles (NVGs), featuring an advanced image intensification technology that allowed him to see the camp's layout with crystal clarity despite the pitch-black conditions. These NVGs, designed for military operations, offered a wide field of view and the ability to detect human figures from significant distances.

Alongside the NVGs, Lima employed a portable thermal imaging monocular, capable of detecting heat signatures through vegetation and light cover. This device was particularly useful for mapping out the locations of guards around the camp as their body heat contrasted sharply with the cooler night environment. By observing these heat signatures, Lima could deduce guard rotation patterns and identify periods of lesser vigilance, critical information for planning a silent infiltration.

After visually surveying the area through the NVGs and thermal monocular, he sketched the camp's structure in his mind, noting the positions of the sentry posts, tents, armouries and potential command centres. He also marked potential entry and exit points that could be exploited for a silent approach.

Silence was the cornerstone of this operation. Even the softest sound risked detection by the camp's sentries. However, the fragile silence was abruptly shattered. A twig, concealed under the leaf litter, snapped under the inadvertent movement of the informer. Instantly, Lima's head snapped towards the source of the sound. The breach of silence was minor. But in the high stakes of covert operations, such trivialities could cascade into disaster.

The immediate aftermath was a tense stillness. Lima froze. A militant sentry, previously a mere heat signature through Lima's thermal imager, pivoted towards the source of the sound. He held a flashlight in his hand. Its beam sliced through the darkness.

Lima assessed his options with the calm precision that was his trademark. Stay hidden and hope the sentry's investigation turned up nothing—or—prepare for a swift, silent countermeasure should their position be compromised. With the militants closing in, his escape route to Indian territory was compromised. After a quick assessment, he decided to take a different but rather risky option.

The plan was audacious in its simplicity: he would use the forest's natural sounds and movements to create a phantom presence, misleading the militants through misdirection rather than confrontation.

He began slithering towards a different direction, once creating a rustle which suggested the movement of wildlife. They leveraged the survival skills honed over their perilous journey to lead the militants on a wild goose chase, away from their actual escape path.

As the militants followed the misleading cues into the deeper forest, their search patterns became erratic, allowing Lima the precious window he needed. This approach, leveraging the environment itself as a tool of deception, required no explosions, no fireworks—only the keen understanding of the land and the discipline to use it to their advantage. Lima's exit was thus a ghostly passage. He left no trace, no disturbance. He moved with efficiency until he made his way back to safety.

***

On the 9th of June, 2015, Major Arjun Singh and his team commenced their covert operation. Army Chief General Dalbir Singh Suhag, who had delayed his trip to the UK for the operation, was overseeing coordination from the Army headquarters. Departing from Imphal, the capital city, Major Singh's team travelled in trucks towards the Naga Hills. Their destination lay beyond the borders, deep within Myanmar's treacherous terrain. The convoy reached the foothills of the Naga Hills, where civilization's footprint faded. Here, the operatives disembarked, their mission transitioning to the next critical phase.

The Naga Hills straddled the border between India and Myanmar. It was a formidable natural fortress. Rising sharply from the surrounding plains, these hills were a part of the larger mountain chain that formed the northeastern boundary of the Indian subcontinent. The terrain here was characterised by steep slopes, deep valleys and fast-flowing rivers. Elevation varied dramatically and offered breathtaking vistas of the surrounding landscape.

The climate of the Naga Hills was as varied as its topography, ranging from subtropical in the lower reaches to temperate in the higher elevations. This variation supported a rich biodiversity, including dense forests of bamboo, teak and rhododendron, which served as home to a wide array of wildlife. The area was alive with the sounds of birds, the rustling of leaves, and the distant roar of waterfalls that was both enchanting and intimidating.

Each member of the unit shouldered a battle load weighing approximately 35 kilograms. This gear, meticulously chosen for both survival and combat, included their standard-issue rifles, ample ammunition, grenades, NVGs, and rations, along with medical supplies and communication devices. The weight of their equipment was a reminder of the stakes at play.

Choosing to navigate through the dense jungle rather than the shorter, more exposed routes, the team embarked on a trek that would test their limits. The humidity within the jungle was oppressive. It wrapped around them like a thick cloak. With each step, their boots sank into the soft earth, the dense canopy above barely allowing any respite from the sun's intensity. The air was heavy with the sounds of the jungle.

The decision to take the longer route through this stifling environment was strategic, maximising stealth and minimising the risk of detection. Despite the physical toll, each member of the team pressed on. They navigated steep inclines and crossed fast-flowing rivers but their resolve remained unshaken.

Major Arjun Singh, with the map unfolded against the trunk of a gnarled tree, traced the route with his finger, his eyes flickering between the paper and the dense jungle ahead. The team huddled close, their breaths shallow, blending with the early morning mist. He pointed to a narrow pass between two towering hills, a natural corridor that would lead them stealthily towards the enemy encampments. With a decisive nod, he folded the map, tucking it away. "This is our path," he whispered, his voice laced with authority and confidence.

The operatives fell in line behind him, each step measured, their eyes scanning the area. Singh led with an instinct honed by years of experience, his senses attuned to the slightest rustle, the faintest scent on the wind. The jungle, with its hidden dangers, seemed to respect their mission, offering passage through its dense underbrush.

As they neared their objective, the tension among the team palpable, Major Singh raised his hand, signalling a halt. With a grave expression, he turned to his second in command, "Initiate radio silence," he ordered, his voice barely above a whisper. The command was met with immediate action; operatives adjusted their radio sets, turning dials until the static hiss faded into silence.

In military parlance, "radio silence" is a tactical directive to cease all electronic communication. This precaution is taken to prevent the enemy from intercepting signals which could reveal the unit's location, strength or intentions. It is a period of enforced silence, a cloak of invisibility in the electronic spectrum, ensuring that the unit moves undetected, ghost-like towards its target. For Major Singh and his team, this silence was a shield that cloaked their final approach in secrecy, allowing them to advance undetected under the cover of the dense foliage.

At the Special Forces Training School, the troops had undergone specialised training in tactics, parachuting, unarmed combat, demolition and survival skills. Their training modules covered jungle warfare, high-altitude warfare, desert warfare and counter-insurgency operations. This phase also included advanced weapons training and operational tactics specific to the Para SF's role in behind-enemy-lines operations. It was now that the training was being applied to the fullest, and Major Singh was leading from the front in the highest traditions of the Indian Army.

Major Arjun Singh and his team continued to navigate the terrain, their bodies drenched in sweat, muscles aching from the relentless march. The dense foliage seemed to conspire against them, branches and underbrush clawing at their gear, obscuring their path, while the thick canopy choked off the light, plunging them into an eerie semi-darkness. The urgency of their mission weighed heavily on their minds, propelling them forward despite the mounting challenges. Delays had plagued their journey from the outset. Time seemed to be slipping away rather quickly.

Suddenly, a rustle in the foliage ahead brought the team to a halt. Years of training and the haunting memories of the Chandel ambush surged through Major Singh's veins, priming him for conflict. His hands tightened around the triggers of rifles, breath held, eyes straining to pierce the gloom. The jungle, however, held its breath.

A group of local hunters emerged from the bushes, oblivious to the drama they had unwittingly entered. Armed with nothing more than traditional bows and machetes, their presence posed a dilemma far removed from the military confrontations Major Singh and his team were accustomed to. Yet, the risk was undeniable; if these men were allowed to pass, the possibility that they might alert the militants loomed large. The entire operation could come crumbling down.

Major Singh's decision came swiftly from his strategic acumen. He ordered a few men of his unit to stay behind, detaining the hunters under their watchful eyes until the mission's conclusion. It was a difficult choice which stretched the limits of their resources and manpower. Yet, it underscored the complexities of operating in such a volatile environment, where the line between civilian and combatant was often blurred.

As the detained hunters sat, watched over by a few armed soldiers, the rest of the team pressed on. As Major Singh and his elite team crept through the dense undergrowth, the dark silhouette of the enemy encampments came into view. Positioned across a narrow clearing, the two camps presented a daunting challenge. The revelation demanded an immediate recalibration of their strategy.

With practised stealth, Singh motioned for his team to disperse, encircling the camps to gather crucial intelligence. They observed the movements within the camps, noting the patrols and the scattered placements of sentries who seemed unaware of the danger that loomed at their doorstep.

Singh, understanding the critical nature of their mission, decided on a three-pronged assault. The plan was bold, requiring precise coordination and timing. Teams Alpha, Bravo and Charlie were to strike simultaneously from the north, south, and west, cutting off any possibility of escape or reinforcement.

As they prepared to set their ambushes, bursts of enemy gunfire echoed through the jungle like thunder. The unexpected gunfire sent a ripple of confusion through Singh's team. But Major Singh was composed. The enemy hadn't spotted them; of that, he was certain. The nature of the gunfire was erratic, purposeless—a tactic designed to provoke a response. It was a gamble on the enemy's part, hoping to flush out any hidden threats by their reaction.

To return fire would be to play into the enemy's hands, revealing their presence and jeopardising the element of surprise they held so dearly. With calm authority, he issued the command to hold any fire.

His team remained motionless, their fingers steady on their triggers but their weapons silent. The random gunfire continued for a few agonising hours before tapering off. The jungle returned to its eerie calm, the threat momentarily abated but the tension undiminished. Singh, with a nod to his team, signalled the continuation of the mission. Vital time had passed in waiting and now the operation could not be delayed anymore. Major Singh made a crucial decision—instead of a three-pronged attack, all teams would now launch a frontal attack.

***

Major Arjun Singh and his team, their silhouettes barely discernible, slid into position along the compound's outer perimeter. The air was tense with expectation, a low hum of distant jungle life the only sound as the team prepared to strike.

Major Singh signalled to his men with a swift hand gesture. The snipers in his team, concealed on the high ground, scanned the compound through their scopes. Each of them focused on a different target. Two sentries stood watch, their flashlights casting fleeting beams across the darkened grounds.

The snipers breathed in unison, their fingers poised on the triggers. A low rustle, two figures moving stealthily along the edge of the compound, and then—two faint pops. The snipers had taken their shots. The sentries fell with barely a sound, their flashlights dropping to the ground and extinguishing on impact.

Major Singh and his team advanced quickly, their combat boots silent against the earth. They reached the compound's fence, a barrier of rusted chain-link with gaps that allowed them entry. The team slipped through, spreading out in a practised formation. Major Singh signalled again, pointing towards the main building where the militants had gathered.

The assault team, armed with assault rifles and grenade launchers, moved swiftly and silently. They flanked the building, pressing their bodies against the rough stone walls. Arjun glanced at his watch, counting down the seconds. It was time.

An explosion shattered the night. A grenade launched from one of the assault rifles hit the building's rear wall, sending a shockwave through the compound. Debris rained down, and a plume of smoke billowed into the sky. The blast was the signal for the snipers to engage.

From their elevated positions, the snipers opened fire. Precision shots rang out, striking the militants who had rushed to investigate the explosion. Arjun's team moved with precision, their assault rifles spitting controlled bursts of fire. Each shot was a calculated strike, designed to neutralise the enemy without causing unnecessary collateral damage.

The militants, caught off guard, scrambled to respond. Rocket launchers appeared on the roof, the telltale glow of their exhaust illuminating the night. One rocket soared over the compound, its trail a blazing arc in the sky. It exploded against the jungle canopy, sending a shower of burning debris to the ground below.

Major Singh's team didn't flinch. They pressed their advantage, advancing towards the main building. Another grenade exploded, this time at the front entrance, creating a gaping hole. Major Singh led the charge, his assault rifle at the ready. His team followed, their movements coordinated and precise.

The firefight escalated as they entered the complex. The crackle of gunfire echoed off the walls, and the sharp tang of gunpowder filled the air. The militants fought back with automatic weapons but Arjun's team was relentless. They cleared one zone after another, using flashbangs to disorient the enemy before storming in with guns blazing.

One of the snipers spotted a militant with a rocket launcher taking aim at the advancing team. With a single shot, he took him down, the rocket launcher clattering to the ground harmlessly. The sniper's cover was blown, and gunfire erupted in his direction. He rolled behind cover, reloading quickly.

Major Singh's team moved deeper into the compound. Chaos intensified with every step. Their mission was clear: cause maximum damage, cripple the enemy's operations, and retreat before reinforcements could arrive. The militants were disoriented, their defensive lines shattered by the sudden assault.

Major Singh ordered his team to scatter within the compound, focusing their firepower on key structures. Grenades were launched into storage areas, sending shockwaves through the complex. Explosions rocked the ground. Smoke billowed into the sky. The militants, caught in the crossfire, stumbled and fell as they tried to mount a defence.

The snipers continued to provide cover from elevated positions, picking off targets with ruthless efficiency. Their shots were swift and precise, each one adding to the confusion below. Arjun watched as a group of militants emerged from a bunker, carrying machine guns and rocket launchers. He signalled to his team, and within moments, the bunker was engulfed in flames from a well-placed grenade.

Forty minutes of absolute mayhem. Major Singh knew it was time to retreat. He raised his hand, signalling his team to fall back. They moved quickly, keeping low to avoid stray bullets. The militants, realising that the attackers were withdrawing, began to regroup.

Major Singh led his team out of the compound. The path was narrow and winding, with overgrown bushes providing some cover. The team moved in a tight formation, weapons at the ready. But the militants were quick to react. A group of them burst through the underbrush, their guns blazing. The firefight intensified again. Muzzle flashes lit up the darkness. The army team returned fire, their assault rifles spitting bullets with deadly accuracy. The militants fell, one after another.

Suddenly, a militant with a machine gun appeared on a nearby hill, his weapon pointed directly at the retreating team. The front man took him out. A single shot rang out, and the militant collapsed, his machine gun slipping from his grasp. Done. *All done.*

The team retreated cautiously, covering each other as they moved. The jungle's dense foliage made it difficult to see more than a few feet ahead. Rustling leaves and distant gunfire echoed in the distance. The team remained focused, their training kicking in as they navigated the treacherous terrain.

Major Singh knew the jungle held its own dangers. He kept his team close, his eyes scanning the darkness for any sign of movement. They had caused significant damage to the enemy but the mission wasn't over until they were safely back on Indian soil. With each step, the team left behind the chaos and destruction they had unleashed. The jungle swallowed the sounds of battle and left only echoes of gunfire. The worst was behind them. They had survived the mayhem. And now, it was a long march home.

***

Inside a briefing room in New Delhi, Defence Minister Manohar Parrikar addressed a meeting. The operation in Myanmar was a success. This was a clear message to anyone who believed they could attack Indian forces and get away with it.

Ajit Doval, his eyes sharp behind his glasses, had played a key role in the operation. He had put the militants on notice. They realised they wouldn't find safe havens across the border any longer. Home Minister Rajnath Singh knew that the nation wanted swift and decisive action. It was delivered. The Indian Army had shown its strength. The operation served as a reminder that our security was non-negotiable.

General Dalbir Singh stood up, his military uniform crisp and adorned with medals. Indian Special Forces were amongst the best in the world. They had carried out the operation with precision and professionalism.

The news of the Indian Army's successful operation against insurgent camps in Myanmar spread quickly, capturing public attention and triggering widespread approval. In the busy streets of Delhi, people gathered around TV screens in electronics shops, watching the breaking news. The bold headlines announced the swift strike, and the reporters' voices echoed through the air, detailing the operation's success.

A small crowd had formed in front of a television shop, watching news and visuals related to the Indian Army's operation. A young man in his twenties, with a smartphone in hand, said to his friend, "It was about time we took action. Those insurgents got what they deserved."

His friend nodded, his eyes fixed on the screen where soldiers in camouflage gear moved through the jungle. "Yeah, this was necessary. We can't let them get away with what they did in Manipur," he replied.

Meanwhile, in the offices of the MEA, diplomats were busy drafting statements to address concerns raised by the Myanmar government. Although Myanmar had been informed about the operation, their officials stressed the importance of respecting international boundaries. A senior diplomat, a middle-aged man in a crisp suit, reviewed the statements, ensuring they struck the right balance between asserting India's right to defend itself and acknowledging Myanmar's sovereignty.

Meanwhile, Major Arjun Singh pushed open the front door of his home, feeling the comforting warmth of familiarity. His wife, a soft smile lighting up her face, greeted him with a gentle hug. "Where have you been all this time?" she asked, her voice filled with genuine curiosity.

Arjun hesitated for a moment, his mind thinking through possible alibis. "Oh, I'd just gone for a long hike in the hills," he replied with a nonchalant shrug.

His wife raised an eyebrow. "Long hike? In the hills?"

Major Arjun Singh nodded.

"Fine," his wife said. "Take a shower. I'll set up dinner."

As Major Arjun Singh stepped into his living room, he felt a sense of relief and warmth that had been absent during his mission. The familiar sounds of his children playing in the background and the scent of his wife's cooking filled the air. It was a contrast to the chaos and tension of the battlefield. He sank into his favourite chair, smiling as his children ran up to greet him. Their laughter was a soothing balm to his weary body. Operation Hot Pursuit was over but the resolve to protect the nation remained steadfast. Forever.

***

The car had now reached Versova. Lucky had provided crucial details about Operation Hot Pursuit. Mr Zaidi took a deep breath, his eyes scanning the surroundings. Versova was a charming blend of the old and new. Quaint, tree-lined streets wound their way past colonial-era bungalows, their facades softened by years of monsoon rains. The aroma of freshly fried fish from local vendors mixed with the salty sea air, creating a unique scent that was distinctly Versova.

"I've always loved this part of the city," Mr Zaidi remarked, his gaze lingering on the fishing village by the beach, where the boats rocked gently with the tide. "It's like a little slice of old Mumbai, untouched by time."

Lucky nodded, smiling at the familiar sights. "It's home. Amidst all the chaos of our missions, it's nice to come back to a place that feels grounded."

Mr Zaidi parked the car by the curb, the engine's hum fading into the background. "You know, Lucky, Operation Hot Pursuit didn't just succeed in its immediate objectives. It set a new benchmark for our counter-terrorism strategies. The combination of precise intelligence and decisive action has redefined how we approach such threats."

"It showed the world that we're capable of striking back swiftly," Lucky said.

"It's a story that will inspire generations to come," Mr Zaidi said. "Every operative, every soldier who hears about Operation Hot Pursuit will know that they're part of a legacy that doesn't back down."

Lucky stepped out of the car, his expression resolute. "And there are more missions to plan, more battles to win."

Lucky walked towards his home, the lights of Versova guiding their way. Mr Zaidi was sure that he would get in touch again with another story of Agent Lima, a character who'd caught Mr Zaidi's attention, and intrigue.

seven

Operation Blind Sparrow

Nestled in a quiet alley off Colaba, was a quaint restaurant that had been serving the city's elite for decades. The walls were adorned with sepia-toned photographs of what was once Bombay, a reminder of the city's rich history. Mr Zaidi entered the establishment and the scent of rich curry enveloped him. He spotted Lucky Bisht at a corner table, already deep in thought.

Lucky waved a hand. "Zaidi saab!"

Mr Zaidi nodded, making his way through the room adorned with old photographs and paintings of Mumbai's bygone era. He sat across from Lucky, who had a serious look on his face.

"Why here, Lucky?" Mr Zaidi asked, curious about the urgency that had brought him to this particular spot.

"I needed a place where we wouldn't be interrupted. Have you heard of Khun Sa?"

Mr Zaidi nodded. "Khun Sa, the notorious opium king of the Golden Triangle. He controlled much of the world's opium trade in the '70s and '80s."

"Exactly," Lucky said. "But he was eventually turned over by the Burmese government to their side. After his surrender in 1996, he provided invaluable intelligence that helped dismantle major drug trafficking networks across Southeast Asia."

"Interesting," Mr Zaidi said. "Turning a high-profile drug lord into an informant."

Lucky smiled faintly. "It reminds me of an operation in which Agent Lima was involved."

"Alright," Mr Zaidi said. "I am all ears."

***

2007: At an undisclosed location, Colonel Sobhraj was in a grim mood. He glared at the photographs on the table as if willing them to provide the answers he sought. His fingers steepled. And a storm brewed inside him. Recently promoted to the rank of a Colonel, he had been tasked with breaking the backbone of the militancy in northeast India. But this battle had taken its pound of flesh. A set of photos depicting lifeless bodies occupied the top of his desk. These were photos of soldiers who'd been ambushed by the NSCN-K, a militant group operating in the northeast.

NSCN was a significant insurgent group operating in northeast India and primarily in the state of Nagaland was formed in 1980. The aim of this organisation was to establish a sovereign Naga state, known as Nagalim, which they envisioned to include Naga-inhabited areas in neighbouring states and even across international borders into Myanmar.

The NSCN split into two major factions in the late 1980s: NSCN-IM (Isak-Muivah) and NSCN-K (Khaplang). Each faction took distinct political stances and strategies. The NSCN-IM was led by Isak Chishi Swu and Thuingaleng Muivah and the NSCN-K was taken over by S.S. Khaplang. All these factions had played central roles in the long-standing Naga conflict.

Colonel Sobhraj opened a file containing details of a mission, codenamed "Operation Blind Sparrow". The file was classified as "secret". Considering the challenging nature of the task at hand, the Colonel had called one of his top operatives to execute the mission. His brooding was interrupted by a knock on the door.

"Come in," the Colonel said.

The door was pushed ajar; and Agent Lima walked in. Back then, Agent Lima was a young operative who had been trained in Israel. He was now ready to be deployed on secret missions. He saluted the senior officer and stood ramrod straight.

"At ease," Colonel Sobhraj said.

Taut creases on the senior officer's forehead were withholding the pressure he was facing from the chief secretary of the Defence Ministry. Three casualties—KIA (Killed In Action)—had demoralised the entire unit. The loss had to be squared off to restore morale and send a stern message to the enemy. Opening the file containing the details of Operation Blind Sparrow, Colonel Sobhraj slid a photograph across the table. Lima picked up the photo and stared at the visage of a young man who was roughly around his age. The man's features had the distinctiveness of the northeast.

"He's John," the Colonel said. "A key member of the NSCN-K group. Very active in Manipur."

Colonel Sobhraj set a clear objective for Agent Lima. Infiltrate enemy lines and capture a key militant leader. Years of violent exchanges had convinced the Agency that militancy couldn't be quelled through force alone. After careful consideration, they devised a strategy to conduct covert missions to support their on-ground forces.

John, a graduate, represented a new era in militant leadership. Rarely seen even by his own comrades, he was considered one of the most strategic minds behind the group's operations. The Agency believed his capture would throw the NSCN-K into chaos and expose its inner workings and future schemes. Colonel Sobhraj produced another photograph and passed it to Lima. This time, Lima was staring at a pretty young woman who appeared to be in her early twenties and a native of the northeast.

"Her name is Ibemhal," Colonel Sobhraj said. "John's girlfriend."

Since John was underground for most of the time, Lima would have to track this girl to get to his target. The three casualties who were martyred had played the catalyst to launching Operation Blind Sparrow. John was known to have in depth information about the location of militants and militant camps in the northeast. If Lima succeeded in trapping John, the Indian forces and agencies would get access to a treasure trove of information which could bring down the various militant movements in the region.

A senior colleague of Lima who was codenamed Victor had been tasked with doing a recon of Manipur to find out a canteen that was *not* run by a local contractor. Such specific orders were issued keeping in mind that local contractors often acted as informants for the army as well as the militants.

"Victor has identified a canteen in Manipur that is run by a Rajasthani contractor named Devi Lal," Colonel Sobhraj told Lima. "Win his confidence and get employed in his canteen. Take the mission forward from there."

Lima marched out of the briefing. He was excited because this was one of his early missions. At the same time, he was also feeling the nerves of not letting this mission fail. Next day, Lima boarded a train bound for Jodhpur, Rajasthan. The canteen contractor's family lived near the Barkatullah Stadium. Going directly to Devi Lal and asking for a job could have raised his suspicions, so Lima had to find a smoother method.

A brief investigation revealed that the contractor's brother was a cricket buff who regularly played on the ground. Lima bought an expensive Kashmir willow cricket bat and went to the playground the next day. The contractor's brother was drawn towards someone in possession of a professional bat.

The brother's eyes lit up as he hefted the Kashmir willow bat, running his fingers along its smooth grain. He turned it over, inspecting the blade closely, then knocked the wood gently with his knuckles, listening for the solid, resonant sound. Satisfied, he took a few practice swings, feeling the perfect balance.

"Where did you get this?" he asked, excitement clear in his voice.

"Picked it up recently," Lima replied with a casual smile, knowing he had captured the brother's interest. "But I don't use it much."

"Why?" asked the brother.

"Because I am new here. Don't have any friends yet."

"Join us," the brother said.

Lima's smile widened as he followed the contractor's brother towards the cricket pitch, stepping into the lively game with anticipation. Each swing of the bat and cheer from the players drew him deeper into their circle. As the game ended and camaraderie filled the air, Lima knew he had not only joined their game but also earned his trust. This successful integration was a crucial move which laid the foundation for the next phase of his mission.

***

Lima would reach the ground each day to put on a convincing act of being a cricket fanatic. Like most Indians, Lima knew a thing or two about straight drives and square cuts. Days passed and the contractor's brother took Lima as his bosom friend. The right time to hit the nail on the head arrived. Lima asked Devi Lal's brother to help him find a job.

"What can you do?" the brother asked.

"I used to work in a kitchen before," Lima said. "I can cook. And I can manage inventory and accounts."

"Really? My elder brother is looking for someone to help him run his canteen in Manipur. In fact, I am visiting him in a few days. Why don't you come along?"

To not appear too eager, Lima showed some hesitation about the location before eventually agreeing to the proposal. They commenced their journey to Manipur by first getting to Delhi, from where they took the train bound for the northeast. They landed in Guwahati and boarded another train towards Dimapur. Then they took a bus to Manipur.

The bus ride was difficult. Militants stationed at certain spots would stop the bus and climb inside. They'd ask each passenger for identification so as to not let any suspicious element sneak into their territory. One of the militants came to where Lima and the contractor's brother were sitting and asked for their identification. Lima had a cover identity card which he duly provided. So far, so good.

But then, the militant demanded that Lima hand him his bag for inspection. Lima controlled his fear. Apart from clothes and other usual stuff of daily use, the bags also contained a miniature knife and a microchip. He had no option but to acquiesce to the militant's demands.

Lima tried to keep his calm as the militant began the checking. Although nondescript in appearance, the bag wasn't ordinary. It was a specially designed bag that had an additional layer stitched inside that could escape even the most scrupulous eyes. The militant found nothing, returned the bag and allowed the bus to pass.

After a long and gruelling journey, Lima reached the canteen and met Devi Lal who was quite a task master. Although he kept those who worked for him on a tight leash, Devi Lal would often throw in some humour to strengthen his bond with the employees. Lima observed, as he was trained to do. The canteen could serve around 30–50 customers at a time. The kitchen was separated from the dining area by a wall.

"Follow me," Devi Lal said.

He led Lima to the room he was going to stay in. Devi Lal slammed his fingers on the switchboard. The only tubelight in the space came on after a few flickers. The dim light cast by the tubelight revealed a small space which was really an excuse for a room.

"Start work from tomorrow," Devi Lal said.

The next morning Lima got ready and went into the kitchen. He was admitted into the cooking department by the main cook, who was a native of Manipur. Lima struck a friendship with him on the pretext of learning the Manipuri language. He learnt from the cook that the locals were fond of jalebis but not many people there knew how to make it.

"I can do it!" Lima said.

"Really?" the cook said. "Show me."

Lima displayed his skills and turned out to be a master jalebi maker. Soon his jalebis became famous among the locals and the army personnel who came to the canteen. He used this opportunity to get close to the army men who visited the canteen regularly. Even the army men did not know of Lima's real identity.

A few days had passed since Lima had started working in the canteen. On a Sunday morning, Lima was serving the canteen's clientele when he saw a girl walk through the door. He recognised her as the girl in the photograph which Colonel Shobhraj had shown to him. Her name was Ibemhal and she was wearing a green kurti and jeans. A big shawl thrown around her neck covered her torso. *She looks like Pooja Bhatt in her prime*, Lima thought.

Lima came up to her. "Your order, ma'am?"

She asked him to bring a plate of *tan, pea dal* and *changang*. Typical Manipuri breakfast. *Tan* referred to the Manipuri version of the Indian puri and *changang* referred to black tea.

"My shop is nearby." Ibemhal smiled. "Deliver it there. Pleas-s-se?"

Twenty minutes later, Lima was at her shop. It was a gift shop, similar to the Archies Gallery he had seen in Delhi. Ibemhal was attending to one of her customers. She gestured to Lima to wait until she was done. Lima glanced at the colourful cards and gifts in the shop. In between, he kept stealing glances at Ibemhal. After the customer was gone, Ibemhal turned her attention towards Lima. She pulled out a few currency notes from the drawer.

They spoke for a brief moment and Lima moved out of the shop so as to not give out a feeling of over-eagerness. He believed that she had taken a liking to him, and he hoped that she'd open up a little more in the upcoming days.

That night, Lima carefully opened the concealed compartment of his bag to retrieve a burner phone. It was a low-cost, prepaid mobile device to be used temporarily and discarded after use. He scanned the surroundings with a cautious eye before dialling Victor to report on his encounter with Ibemhal. The canteen was mostly deserted at this late hour, but the unpredictable Devi Lal could still make an unexpected appearance.

"Did you learn anything from her?" Victor asked.

"She runs a gift shop not far from the canteen," Lima said. "Details to follow."

"Fine. Be cautious."

Lima carefully returned the phone to its hidden compartment and secured it. Exhausted from the day's efforts, he stretched out on the narrow bed, his body tensing before finally relaxing into the sparse comfort. As he drifted off to sleep, Lima's mind remained alert, half-expecting the sound of footsteps or the creak of the door that might signal danger. But the night remained still for most parts.

***

Next week, Lima kept stepping out from the clamour of the kitchen to the dining hall every ten minutes under the guise of seeking fresh air. On his fourth exit, pretending to gasp for breath, his eyes met Devi Lal's penetrating gaze. Lima was about to retreat into the kitchen when Ibemhal entered the canteen. It was crucial to forge a closer link with her. She held the key to John. She wanted to place a big order for her upcoming party.

"Looks like a celebration is in the air," Lima said casually.

"My friends are coming over," Ibemhal said, her voice light but not quite convincing.

Friends? Lima's thoughts flickered to the possibility of John being among them. He had to find a way to grow his proximity to her. He thought language could be a good bond in that direction.

"Could you teach me the local dialect?" Lima asked. "It's challenging to get by without it."

Ibemhal laughed softly. "Meet me tomorrow at my shop."

Then she turned to leave. Lima waved until she was out of sight, his smile a mask that hid his strategic intent. As he spun towards the kitchen, he almost collided with Devi Lal, whose frown quickly dissolved into a sly grin. They shared a brief, knowing chuckle, a moment of light-hearted camaraderie before Devi Lal's tone hardened.

"Stop laughing. And get back to work," he commanded.

The next day, Agent Lima made sure that Devi Lal was nowhere around before he convinced the main chef that he needed to go out for some work. He wanted to go and meet Ibemhal.

"I'll get you a bottle of beer when I return," Lima said.

The offer was a good one for the main chef who loved his beer. He agreed to cover for Lima. Lima snuck out of the kitchen and landed at Ibemhal's shop. She took him to a nearby garden where Lima sat across from her and they began chatting. During the long conversation that ensued, Lima deliberately made some references that would impress upon her that he was privy to the operations that the army was undertaking in that area.

"How do you know all this?" Ibemhal asked.

"A lot of army officers visit our canteen," Lima said. "I overheard a few of them talking the other day." He needed to mention something that would make her think of John. "A militant who surrendered recently has been offered refuge by the Army. Otherwise, he was a sitting duck."

It wasn't as absurd as it sounded. Across the country, there were instances of intelligence agencies using former militants to fight insurgencies. It had been done in Jammu & Kashmir and even in Naxal areas.

"The military does that?" Ibemhal asked.

"The military is accommodating the insurgents who turn themselves in. Not sure how long this amnesty will last."

Ibemhal was lost in her thoughts for a while before telling Lima that she needed to leave. Lima knew that the trick had worked and that he had got her thinking. The two bid goodbye and she left; still brooding. Later, Lima conveyed his progress to the base through his phone to Victor who reiterated the importance of being on alert and wary of doing or saying anything that could lead anyone to suspect him.

Lima was sure that he had got Ibemhal intrigued and that she would definitely be there in the canteen the next day. His assumption turned out to be true. In fact, she reached the canteen earlier than he had expected. Perhaps, she wanted to pursue the conversation he had started yesterday.

Lima was more than happy to let that happen. He sneaked out of the canteen with her to speak in a more private setting. Ibemhal steered the conversation towards the topic of insurgency in Manipur. She sang praises for S.S. Khaplang, who was also called Baba by his followers.

"Baba is fighting for our rights," she said.

Lima came back to the kitchen after the end of their conversation that day in a state of confusion. Ibemhal's stance of holding Khaplang and militancy in high regard cast doubt on his assumptions that she would contemplate turning John in. He got in touch with Victor, who suggested that Lima should make her feel the *fear*—of a loved one's death. It was one of the scariest things in the world. Lima understood what Victor was asking Lima to do and he conceived a strategy to employ when he met with Ibemhal next time.

The next day, Lima thought of going to her shop to see her. But Devi Lal was concerned about what he thought was a blooming romance between Lima and Ibemhal brewing during Lima's duty hours. He was keeping an eye over Lima, and the latter decided to use another trick to meet Ibemhal. A teenage boy was employed in the canteen to get vegetables from the market using a Tata Tempo.

"Listen," Lima whispered to the boy. "Let me take the tempo today."

"The boss will kill me," the boy said.

Lima pulled out a bunch of notes from the pocket of his jeans and stuffed it in the boy's shirt. The boy handed over the tempo's keys in return, allowing him to go get vegetables that day. Lima drove the Tata to Ibemhal's shop. She was surprised to find him there and asked him what was so urgent that he came to see her.

"The errand boy is on leave today," Lima said. "In his place, I am going to get some veggies from the market." He paused. "What do you call cucumbers in Manipuri?"

Ibemhal laughed and understood that Lima was trying to strike a conversation with her. She invited him inside her shop. The conversation drifted from learning Manipuri to the treatment of the captured militants by the army. All the time, Lima was brainwashing Ibemhal into believing that the only chance a militant had, if he wanted to live, was to surrender to the armed forces. He returned to the canteen soon after, once again leaving Ibemhal with something to ruminate about.

Ibemhal had now fallen totally into Lima's trap which resulted in their meetings becoming more frequent. Days wore on wherein Lima and Ibemhal would engage in intense conversations. Lima would deliberately lay emphasis on the military's tendency to show leniency to the rebels who turned themselves in. At the same time, he would also recount to her the tales of the militants who met an unpleasant end due to their insistence on engaging in seditious activities.

Lima updated Victor about what had transpired during his last few meetings with Ibemhal. Victor was convinced that any more approach from Lima's would be overkill.

"You've played your hand," he told Lima. "Let's see if she falls for it."

Finally, Ibemhal invited Lima to the party she had planned. He did not know what to make of that. Was it a ruse to trap him or was it really an invitation to a house party? Was John on the guest list? With all these questions in his mind, Lima accepted the invitation. It was his chance to get a glimpse of Ibemhal's inner circle.

"Get a few bottles of liquor from the army stock," Ibemhal told him.

Lima managed to get one from the CSD canteen. In the evening, Ibemhal picked up Lima and led him to a path that led down the mountains. They kept walking for a long time and Lima started to feel tired. At last, after walking for nearly half an hour they reached her house and Lima found a group of men sitting there already, waiting. Lima did not have to think twice to realise that they were militants.

Lima had been assured by Victor that he was always under the careful watch of the Agency. He wanted to believe Victor, but he had his concerns. The Agency had not given him permission to carry weapons on this mission, because discovery of those by any chance would surely lead to Lima's capture by the enemy and his eventual death.

So what if I can't keep firearms? Lima thought. He carried a small knife tucked under the sole of his shoes. The knife had to be pulled out with the same force as it had been driven into the guts of the victim if the attacker did not want the knife to come out tangled with the person's entrails. Lima felt comfortable knowing that the knife was inside his shoes. He sat down with the militants.

"Let me get you some *jal*," Ibemhal told Lima.

Contrary to Lima's assumptions, the jal in question was not water but an alcoholic drink prepared from rice water, just like the famous Sake of Japan. Lima's hesitancy was growing by the minute. What if the drink was poisoned? Ibemhal poured the jal for him using the same jug from which she filled her glass. This erased Lima's reluctance. He took a sip, and felt its taste in his throat.

"Stay for dinner," Ibemhal told Lima.

He wanted to turn down Ibemhal's request but couldn't bring himself to do that. He was hoping that John would turn up and he would get a glimpse of his target, in flesh and blood.

"Take off your shoes," Ibemhal said. "Be comfortable."

Lima felt an acute sense of awareness of the knife concealed in his shoes at that moment and quickly created a diversion. While he was busy attending to Ibemhal's queries, he also cast intermittent glances at the militants who had huddled around the lamp and seemed to be over-excited about something.

"Is the army going to conduct any special operation soon?" Ibemhal asked Lima.

"For sure," Lima said. "Anyone who wants to live must surrender."

Lima was confident that Ibemhal was now seriously contemplating surrendering her boyfriend to the military. She paused and did not talk for a second or two. The militants hooted and cheered in the distance and Lima looked at them curiously, wondering what they were up to. That's when one of the militants came to them holding a big towel that contained dead wasps. He said something to Ibemhal in Manipuri and left. Lima realised that all the commotion that took place around the lamp was about eating the wasps.

"What did he say?" Lima asked Ibemhal.

"He told me to fry them," Ibemhal said, pointing at the dead flies.

A lump formed in his throat. "Fry? For what?"

"Dinner."

Lima could not believe his ears. He made an excuse and got the hell out of there before he got served with fried wasps.

***

In the exchange that took place with Victor that night, Lima was ordered to make more trips to Ibemhal's place to gather clues related to John. To achieve that objective, Lima stopped his visits to Ibemhal's shop for the next ten days. He was hoping that Ibemhal would come seeking him, and eventually she did.

"Where have you been?" she asked.

"Things have been busy here," Lima said. "The special operation has commenced. Twelve militants have surrendered already."

"How is the army treating them?"

"They are alive, and breathing, and well fed," Lima said. "What more can one want?"

Ibemhal's mind seemed to be racing towards something. Lima thought this was the perfect opportunity to pop the golden question.

"Do you know someone who wants to surrender?" Lima said.

Ibemhal nodded nervously. Lima told her that he knew a senior from the military with whom he could arrange a meeting for her. She agreed and Lima introduced her to Victor. Ibemhal was reassured that the surrendered militants are not subjected to torture or any kind of harsh treatment.

"In fact, they get the same food as us," Victor explained.

Ibemhal came out of the meeting with a pondering demeanour and Lima could see that Victor's words had deeply impacted her. He was about to speak to her when her phone rang. She carried a Panasonic mobile phone which she always made sure of keeping close to her. Lima was of the opinion that she talked with John on this phone but he couldn't bet on that. She took the call in front of Lima and spoke to someone in Manipuri. Lima tried hard to decipher the conversation but he couldn't. His knowledge of Manipuri was still limited.

She ended the call. "I need to go," she said.

"We can talk about this more later," Lima said.

"Come to my shop tomorrow."

"It is better if we have the discussion in a more private setting," Lima said.

"Okay," she said. "At my place then?"

"Fine. At seven?"

"Get some booze, please," Ibemhal said. "I need a drink. Or two."

That night, Lima was handed another mic by Victor which

was to be clipped inside his shirt while visiting Ibemhal's house the next day. It was a mic used to snoop on the conversations that Lima would have with anyone at Ibemhal's place. Lima was expecting John to show up at the house now that she had spoken with Victor and had followed it up with a phone call wherein she spoke to someone in Manipuri. In addition to the knife inside his shoes, Lima had to be cautious about the mic inside his shirt.

The next day, he reached Ibemhal's house at the fixed time. It was a small house that had only one bedroom. The living room had a modest-sized bed which was occupied by an elderly couple whom Lima took as Ibemhal's parents. Lima cast a sweeping glance at the house and discovered that its inhabitants nurtured a deep attachment to their tradition. They had refused to sacrifice their tradition at the altar of modernity. Then Lima's eyes fell on a frail and wasted figure that sat at the foot of the bed and swayed back and forth.

"He is my younger brother," Ibemhal said. "Unfortunately, he is a junkie."

Lima was reminded of the drug menace in the region which was further contributing to the law and order issues and also funding the militancy in the state.

In 2007, northeast India faced a severe drug crisis due to its proximity to the Golden Triangle, a major drug-producing area comprising Thailand, Myanmar and Laos. The region's prolific production of opium and synthetic drugs like methamphetamines significantly fuelled the drug problems in northeast India. States like Manipur and Nagaland saw higher rates of substance abuse compared to other Indian regions.

The porous borders with Myanmar facilitated drug trafficking, exacerbated by local insurgent groups. High rates of injecting drug use led to widespread HIV infections. The societal impact was devastating, with increased mental health issues and community breakdowns. Ibemhal's brother was also a casualty of this fiasco.

Dinner consisted of chicken and rice, much to Lima's great relief. Ibemhal called for a drinking session. Lima brought out the bottle he had got from the canteen from the military stock and kept it on the table besides the traditional alcohol laid out by Ibemhal.

Lima made sure that he did not indulge too much lest it be a trope by Ibemhal to sedate him so that John would find it easy to kill him whenever he decided to come out of hiding. He had the constant suspicion that Ibemhal and John had discovered his identity and were toying with him, even if that weren't necessarily true.

All this time Lima could not shake off the feelings of threat posed by the mic he had worn inside his shirt. Ibemhal then invited Lima to her room. There was a similar-sized bed in the room and a small bureau. The room was full of stuff that appeared handmade and which Lima had noticed being present at Ibemhal's shop as well.

A couple of pumpkins with scary eyes and a creepy smile were kept next to the bureau. Ibemhal told Lima that she was fond of Halloween and loved painting faces on pumpkins and keeping them in her room. Apart from Ibemhal's fascination with painting and decorating, entering her room also gave Lima the chance to learn something that was part of her culture. Ibemhal came and sat close to Lima, resting her head on his shoulders. Lima felt a bit awkward.

"You have a problem with this?" Ibemhal said.

"No," Lima said. "But your brother might have one."

"He won't come here."

"Why?"

"Brothers never enter their sister's room in our culture."

Lima found the social norm interesting. He excused himself and walked out of the room to get his shoes, which he had finally removed. He kept them near the door frame.

"Why are you so fussy about the shoes?" Ibemhal asked, slurring under the effect of the alcohol.

"They are a gift from someone," Lima said.

"Girlfriend?"

Lima nodded. In reality, he had purchased the shoes from Palika Bazar in Delhi at a clearance sale.

"Is she beautiful?" Ibemhal asked.

"Very," Lima said, conjuring up an imaginary face in his head.

"More beautiful than me?" Ibemhal said, her face flushing red.

Before Lima could come up with an answer, she bent over, with a pout on her lips. Lima could feel her breath on his face, and the whiffs of whiskey. Unsure what to do, Lima closed his eyes but realised that his lips had also pouted in anticipation. And then...nothing.

Lima opened his eyes to see that Ibemhal had conked off on the bamboo mat which was spread on the floor. In the faint glow of the light cast by the lamp hung outside in the porch area, Lima surveyed however much of the room he could without venturing too far away from his sleeping place or bumping into anything that would wake up Ibemhal. He also took a quick peek into her phone. He was disappointed to find no recent entries in her call logs. In fact, there were no calls, incoming as well as outgoing, for that day. He was perplexed.

Ibemhal made slight movements. Lima swiftly replaced the phone next to her pillow and skipped to his place. The night passed without anything remarkable taking place and Lima came back to the canteen the next morning with nothing that would lead them to John. He was sure that Victor was running out of patience. His fears were proven right.

"The operation is taking longer than expected," Victor told Lima. "She is indeed John's girlfriend. We should take her into custody and force her to spill John's whereabouts."

"She won't speak a word under duress," Lima said. "I need a few more days to make a breakthrough."

"We are running out of time," Victor said. "Her junkie brother will know a thing or two about John. Let's pick him up."

Lima replied with a hesitated "yes" and ended the call. There was a certain risk in picking up Ibemhal's brother. If John became aware that the agencies had picked up one of his acquaintances, he would become extra-cautious. But Lima had to execute the orders. He drifted to sleep in the midst of making elaborate plans of how to pick up Ibemhal's brother and bring him to a safehouse where Victor would interrogate him. And what would happen if Ibemhal's brother did not spill any beans? Would he be allowed to go? Or was there something worse in store for him?

***

The next day, Lima woke up and went about his business with different plans of picking up Ibemhal's brother playing in his head. He would keep dropping one plan in the favour of a new one which he would deem to be better in terms of execution. Unsure of which plan to prioritise, Lima went to Ibemhal's shop with the intention of taking some more time to finalise his plan of action. However, nothing could have prepared him for what was going to happen at the shop.

A crowd had assembled near the shop's downed shutters. Never since he had known Ibemhal had he seen such a gathering at her shop. Surely, they aren't customers, he thought.

"What's the matter?" he asked them in a broken combination of Manipuri and English.

"Don't you know?" a man in the group replied. "The girl's brother died."

Lima's jaw nearly hit the floor. On further inquiry, he learnt that the body was at the local hospital. Lima bounded down the same curved path the men had pointed in. On reaching the hospital, he found Ibemhal sitting outside the postmortem room. Wailing. Crying. Howling. The body of her brother had just been released to her. Lima consoled Ibemhal and then moved towards the stretcher on which the body was laid.

He lifted the shroud. One look at the bullet wounds on the body's head and chest were all Lima needed to determine that the killer had shot him from close range. Lima assisted Ibemhal with conducting the funeral rites and then rushed to contact Victor for a briefing.

"The rival NSCN faction did him," Victor told Lima over the phone. "Perhaps, this will speed up John's surrender."

Victor's prediction came true as her brother's killing became the tipping point for Ibemhal. On December 12th, 2007, Ibemhal met Lima and confessed that she wanted her boyfriend, John, to surrender to the military. Lima consulted with Victor again during their nocturnal conversations on the phone. Victor instructed Lima to tell Ibemhal that he wouldn't take her words seriously until she called John in front of him, and had that conversation with her boyfriend in Lima's presence. Lima brought up this topic during her next meeting with Ibemhal.

"Okay," Ibemhal said. "Follow me."

Lima did not know what to expect but did as he was told. Ibemhal led him straight to her room. Lima was becoming increasingly curious to know the means of communication with which Ibemhal kept in touch with John. He had studied her house during his last visit but couldn't find anything that would act as a device in disguise capable of establishing a connection with John; and it was certainly not her Panasonic phone.

To his utmost surprise, Ibemhal thrust her hand into one of the Halloween pumpkins and retrieved a wireless set that left Lima staring at it with his mouth wide open. It was a device that far surpassed the technology that the Agency possessed at the time. It was a phone-sized wireless set. Lima heaved a sigh of relief as he saw that she was genuinely interested in John's surrender and wasn't deceiving him all this while.

She kept talking over the wireless in Manipuri for a while. Lima could comprehend enough to understand that John was telling Ibemhal that he would be there on 25 December to celebrate Christmas with her before turning himself in. Ibemhal ended her conversation with John and stuffed the wireless back into its hiding place.

Lima praised her decision and bravery before bidding her goodbye. "You did the right thing," he said.

Back at the canteen, he went about his work and kept in touch with Ibemhal to make sure there was no change in her plan to bring John to the surrender table.

Christmas was around the corner. The small Christian community of Manipur that mainly belongs to the two tribes, Ukhrul and Kuki, flocked the markets in preparations for the coming celebration. But Ibemhal was gripped with overwhelming concern regarding John's entry into the village and making it to her place safely. She wasn't prepared to lose the man she loved when she hadn't yet healed from the wounds inflicted by her brother's death.

Lima spoke to Victor who decided that the Agency would deploy a contingent of soldiers around Ibemhal's house as well as the shop in a discreet manner on the day they were expecting John, i.e., 25 December.

John, however, arrived a day earlier than expected. Ibemhal conveyed this information to Lima so that he could meet them at the shop in a few hours and arrange for the surrender. After spending time with John, Ibemhal took him to her shop. He was supposed to hide there until Lima and Victor would arrive to close the final phase of the surrender.

Ibemhal pulled the sliding door of the shop shut for the sake of privacy. Topics of their discussions varied from the upcoming surrender to the plans they had in mind to celebrate the day. Close to the end of their conversation, their gaze met. Ibemhal and John leaned forward to share an intimate moment when there was a knock on the door. Ibemhal wondered if the army men had arrived early to take John, but was surprised to see a small boy standing outside the door.

"The shop's closed," Ibemhal said, without opening the door completely.

"Please sister," the boy said, "I want to buy some decorations for my Christmas tree."

John gestured at her to go ahead. Ibemhal opened the door. The boy gambolled in and picked a few cards of his choice, made the payment and went away. Ibemhal watched affectionately as the boy went out of sight. She was about to shut the door when a couple of men blocked the slide, the barrel of their guns pointed at her.

"Get down!" John shouted, pushing Ibemhal behind a display stand.

The first militant, a tall man with a scar running down his cheek, stepped inside. He was followed by another, stockier and equally menacing. John lunged at the tall man, grabbing the barrel of his rifle and forcing it upwards. The weapon discharged, sending a burst of bullets into the ceiling. Plaster rained down. And the acrid smell of gunpowder filled the air.

The stocky militant aimed his rifle at John, but with surprising speed, John grabbed a heavy wooden shelf and swung it towards him. The shelf collided with his arm, causing him to drop the weapon. John and the militant grappled furiously, each trying to gain the upper hand. The scarred man was strong, but John, fuelled by desperation, managed to twist the rifle out of his grasp. He swung the butt of the rifle at the man's head, landing a solid blow that sent him sprawling to the ground.

Just as John turned to help Ibemhal, he felt a searing pain in his side. He looked down to see blood blossoming from a wound, the result of a knife the stocky militant had managed to draw. John staggered but remained upright, driven by sheer will. He tackled the stocky militant, and they both fell to the floor, locked in a deadly struggle. The room echoed with the sounds of their fierce combat—grunts, the clash of metal, and the splintering of wood.

Meanwhile, Victor and Lima were driving towards the shop to pick up John. As they approached the shop, they saw flashes of gunfire through the broken windows. Lima's heart pounded. Lima and Victor pulled out their weapons and fired from the cover of their vehicle. But they had limited firepower in the form of pistols while the militants were carrying assault rifles. The militants had fired enough rounds to leave John heavily wounded. He wasn't moving. Sensing that their mission had been accomplished, the militants beat a hasty retreat.

Victor rushed to Ibemhal's side, checking for a pulse. His face fell. "She's gone," he muttered.

John lay nearby, breathing raggedly. Lima checked his pulse. "Let's get him to the hospital," he screamed.

Together, Lima and Victor carried John out of the shop and into the jeep. As they raced towards the nearest hospital, Lima kept pressure on John's wound, hoping to stem the bleeding. The drive felt endless, each minute stretching into an eternity. At the hospital, they were met by a flurry of medical personnel. John was whisked away into surgery, leaving Lima and Victor in the sterile, fluorescent-lit waiting room. Lima sank into a chair. He glanced at Victor, who gave a nod of grim determination. The mission had taken a heavy toll but finally, they had John in their custody.

***

John miraculously recovered in the hospital. He was later moved to an Army camp. Eventually, the day came when Colonel Sobhraj himself arrived to speak with John. In a small, private room, John stood upright. Pain and regret etched deeply into his face. Colonel Sobhraj, with his stern yet compassionate demeanour, entered the room and took a seat.

"I never thought I'd see this day," John said quietly, his voice heavy with remorse. "I made a mistake. Joining the militants…it was wrong."

Sobhraj nodded, his eyes reflecting a deep understanding. "We all make mistakes, John. The important thing is what we do to rectify them. You have a chance now. Use it well."

John's recovery marked the beginning of a new chapter. Integrated into the army's intelligence unit, he provided crucial information about the militants' operations, their hideouts and their strategies. His insights led to the capture of many insurgents and the destruction of numerous hideouts in Manipur and the neighbouring states. Each successful operation was a step towards restoring peace in the troubled region.

Lima would also often meet John during his stay in the northeast. Sometimes, they would meet in quiet, secluded spots, away from the chaos of their operations. Their conversations were filled with reflections on the past and hopes for the future. Despite the camaraderie and the progress they made, a profound sadness lingered in John's eyes. They even conducted a few operations together. One evening, after another successful raid, Lima and John shared a private conversation.

"You've done well, John," Lima said. "Your information has been invaluable."

"As much as I destroy them," John said, "I will never be able to avenge *her*."

Lima's gaze softened. "Grief is a heavy burden, John. But remember, her sacrifice has not been in vain. She believed in you, and she helped you find your way back. Honour her memory by continuing to do good."

John nodded, staring into the distance. The future held the promise of redemption and the hope of a better tomorrow. And as the night embraced them, the two men sat in quiet companionship, bound by their shared past and the unspoken vow to free the region from the plague of violence.

***

Back in the perfect ambience restaurant in Colaba, Mr Zaidi absorbed the gravity of Lucky's tale. The story of John's transformation from a militant to a valuable informant echoed the complexities of war.

"John helped us dismantle significant portions of the NSCN-K," Lucky said. "But the scars, both physical and emotional, ran deep."

"It's incredible how someone can turn their life around so drastically," Mr Zaidi said.

"Indeed." Lucky agreed. "John's story, much like Khun Sa's, shows that even the most hardened individuals can find a path to redemption. It's never easy. But it is possible."

The restaurant was slowly emptying as patrons finished their meals and left.

Mr Zaidi leaned back in his chair, reflecting on the narrative that had unfolded. These stories were a reminder of the human cost of conflict and the power of change. The two men shook hands.

"Until next time, Lucky," Mr Zaidi said.

"Yes-sir," Lucky said.

Lucky stepped out into the Mumbai night, leaving Mr Zaidi to ponder about the depths of the story he had just heard, and the many untold stories that lay hidden in the layers of conflict.

eight

Operation Black Widow

Mr Zaidi and Lucky Bisht were taking a stroll in a garden near Ghatkopar. The city's skyline stretched out in a glittering display of lights. The night air was cool but carried the sounds of traffic and incessant horns. Potted plants lined the edges of the pathway, their leaves rustling gently in the breeze. They were discussing one of Mossad's most famous female agents.

"Sylvia Raphael," Mr Zaidi said, "became renowned for her skills in undercover operations and assassinations."

Born in South Africa, Sylvia was recruited by Mossad and turned into a lethal agent. Sylvia was a master of infiltration and disguise. She had the ability to blend in, gain trust and strike with precision. She was part of "Wrath of God", a covert operation launched by Mossad which was aimed at eliminating those responsible for the massacre of Israeli athletes during the 1972 Munich Olympics.

Sylvia was involved in several high-risk operations, often working alone or in small teams. Her ability to navigate hostile environments and execute missions made her a legend in the world of espionage. She was part of a group of Mossad agents who killed Ahmed Bouchiki, a Morocco-born waiter, in Lillehammer, Norway, on 21 July 1973 after mistaking him for Ali Hassan Salameh, the mastermind behind the Munich massacre. This operation became infamous as the Lillehammer affair. She was imprisoned and later released, but the ordeal took a toll on her health. She passed away in 2005.

"It's incredible how much influence one agent's legacy can have on future operations," Lucky said.

"Indeed. Sylvia's methods and principles were a mark of her genius."

"There's an operation where Agent Lima had to seek assistance from a female operative who was, perhaps, as deadly as Sylvia Raphael."

Mr Zaidi raised an eyebrow, intrigued.

Lucky was poised to begin. "It started from a bar in Tel Aviv..."

***

The year teetered on the brink of 2009. In the confines of a bar in Tel Aviv, Sherry Ramsey sat alone with her attention ostensibly on the brimming glass of Bloody Mary on her table. Her dark hair, cut in a sleek bob, framed her sharp features. A light sprinkle of freckles dusted her nose and cheeks, giving her an air of youthful innocence. She wore a fitted leather jacket paired with dark jeans. Her posture was relaxed, yet there was a coiled tension in her muscles. Her eyes frequently darted to the entrance, primed for the visitor she was expecting.

Sherry's life was filled with clandestine meetings and high-stakes operations. In the world of espionage, she was known as the black widow, after the species of female spiders who devour their male counterparts after mating. A former Mossad operative,

Sherry had a reputation built on a foundation of impeccable fieldwork and unshakeable nerves. She had orchestrated the extraction of a key informant from the heart of Tehran, and her subtle manipulation of a major arms deal in Eastern Europe had averted what could have been a prolonged conflict. Each mission had honed her skills, making her an asset in the world of international espionage. It was these skills that Agent Lima wanted to put to use as he entered the bar and walked towards Sherry's table. They made small talk before getting down to business.

"The target is a high-profile militant leader in India," Lima said. "And the mission is high risk."

"High risk equals high money," Sherry said.

"How much?"

The slight narrowing of Sherry's eyes spoke of calculated thoughts. She quoted a price that roughly translated to one and half crores in Indian currency.

"Non-negotiable," she said before Lima could even utter a word.

Lima paused, the amount was steep, higher than what his superiors had hoped. Yet, securing Sherry's services was crucial. Her past operations had amply demonstrated her effectiveness and her ability to disappear without a trace—an essential quality for the delicate nature of this mission. He put in a call to Colonel Sobhraj who was taken by surprise on hearing the quote. This mission would cost a significant portion of the secret services fund. But after much consideration and further consultation with his superiors, Sobhraj gave the green light.

"Agreed," Lima told Sherry. "But the timeline is tight."

"The job will take fifteen days," Sherry said. "I'll land in India after 50 per cent of the advance is transferred to an account in Kuwait."

Their conversation wrapped quickly after that. Sherry gave

Lima the details of the account where the advance was to be transferred. As Sherry stood up to leave, her posture was confident. The seasoned operative was ready to engage in a high-stakes game. Lima was aware that he had just set in motion a plan that could stir tensions in the delicate peace in the northeast. But for now, he had to trust the skills of the agent he had hired and hope that the gamble would pay off.

Who was the high-profile target of this mission? What had caused him to appear on the Agency's hitlist? And why had Agent Lima shown up in a bar in Tel Aviv? The roots to the answers of such questions were buried in an event which occurred two weeks ago in the remote town of Sugnu, Manipur.

***

Two weeks ago: Sugnu in Manipur was a frontier town which lay immersed in the dense whispers of India's border with Myanmar. An outpost marked the final stretch of Indian territory before the land dissolved into the forests of Myanmar. Here, a company of the Indian Army was stationed as a vigilant presence in a volatile zone. This unit, comprising about sixty soldiers, was entrenched in a routine that spanned the gamut from mundane to high alert.

At the nearby military camp, four soldiers were huddled around a battered carrom board nestled under a makeshift awning. Laughter punctuated the air, mingling with the soft clatter of wooden coins and the slap of the striker. "Raj, your aim in carrom is as bad as your shooting—always missing the mark!" Lance Naik Joshi said.

The joke prompted a burst of laughter from the others and momentarily blunted the sharpness of constant vigilance. Unseen, nestled in the dense brush bordering the camp, a pair of eyes was watching the scene with cold calculation. Hidden beneath a cloak of foliage, a militant reconnaissance leader noted the low presence of soldiers at the camp. He used his radio to connect with his handler.

"There are fewer soldiers in the camp today," the militant said.

"Prepare to move in," the handler ordered.

Most of the soldiers in the camp had been dispatched as a Road Opening Party (ROP. An ROP is a security and reconnaissance detail primarily used by military and police forces in regions where there is a high risk of attacks, such as ambushes or landmines. The primary function of an ROP is to ensure that roads and pathways are safe and secure for the movement of convoys, military units and civilians. This is especially critical in conflict zones or areas with ongoing insurgent activity.

Back at the carrom board in the camp, Havildar Singh lined up his shot, oblivious to the danger encroaching their perimeter. He flicked the striker with precision. The coin shot into the pocket, eliciting a round of impressed murmurs.

As the soldiers revelled in their game, the militants made their decisive move. Slithering closer to the wire fence, they used bolt cutters to break through. With a gap just wide enough to pass through, the two insurgents exchanged a look of determination and slipped through the camp's defences. Inside, the sudden silence following a particularly loud bout of laughter felt ominous. Lance Naik Joshi, ever alert despite the relaxed setting, paused before aiming his next shot. His eyes narrowed.

"Did you hear that?" he said.

"Probably just a monkey in the bushes," Havildar Singh said.

But Singh's hand subconsciously moved to the sidearm resting by his side. His instincts proved right. The militants, having breached the perimeter, wasted no time in opening fire. Harsh cracks of automatic gunfire tore through the camp. Bullets whizzed past the awning.

"Fire," Havildar Singh shouted.

He dived for cover as the others scrambled for their weapons. Havildar Singh fired off rounds in the direction of the attackers. The soldiers were jolted from camaraderie into chaos. The thud of carrom coins falling to the ground was drowned out by falling bodies, hitting the dirt. The attack was swift. Brutal. The four soldiers now lay still, their lives extinguished in an instant.

Echoes of gunfire faded but the camp was thrust into a frenetic burst of activity. Alerts were sounded. Reinforcements rallied. The camp's perimeter was secured once again. The grimness of military engagement had substantially breached a thin line between peace and violence in this remote borderland.

Ripples of the ambush in Sugnu were felt deeply across Manipur. The quiet rhythm of daily life was unsettled. The news of the attack travelled swiftly, stirring a mix of fear and uncertainty. It was clear that the Indian forces would retaliate with an iron glove.

In the heart of Manipur's rugged terrain lay 57 Deep Mount, i.e., 57 Mountain Division of the Indian Army which specialised in mountain warfare and counterinsurgency. It was here, amidst the austere beauty of steep cliffs and dense forests, that the General Operation Commander (GOC) held command. The GOC, a figure both respected and weathered by the trials of military leadership, was briefed with a grave urgency.

The Army's response was swift and decisive. The focus of their scrutiny was the militant group KYKL, known for its active insurgence in the region. KYKL remained committed to the establishment of an independent socialist state in the region. Formed in 1994 through the amalgamation of various insurgent factions, the KYKL's activities ranged from armed engagements with security forces to social reform campaigns, making them a complex player in the ongoing conflict dynamics of Manipur.

A cordon-off search operation was immediately launched, saturating the area with troops and surveillance. Soldiers combed through the undergrowth, their boots pressing into the soft earth as they searched for any clue, any trace that might lead them to the assailants. Yet, despite their exhaustive efforts, the attackers seemed to have vanished into the very air, leaving behind a trail as elusive as smoke.

The KYKL's vehement denials of involvement did little to sway the Army's suspicions. Intelligence reports, intercepts and the pattern of previous engagements painted a different picture—one where the lines of innocence and guilt were blurred by shades of guerrilla tactics. Over the ensuing days, the military campaign against KYKL intensified. Soldiers, guided by the grim motivation of their fallen comrades, dismantled several hideouts attributed to the militant group. Each destroyed hideout was a blow to the insurgent infrastructure—a disruption of their logistics and morale. As the operations drew to a close, the landscape of Manipur bore the scars of conflict and the tentative hope of resolution. But another twist in the tale was about to emerge.

***

During the time when the militants ambushed a camp at Sugnu, Agent Lima was deployed within the clandestine Military Intelligence (MI) unit of the Indian Army. The MI's temporary outpost, strategically located a few kilometres outside Imphal, was a nexus of activity against a backdrop of both historical strife and the vibrant chaos of nature.

The roots of the MI unit stretched back through decades of evolving warfare, adapting from the straightforward intelligence collection of the World War II era to modern challenges such as cyber threats, counter-insurgency and counter-terrorism. The

MI's operations were crucial in navigating through the choppy waters of insurgent dynamics and regional politics.

Agent Lima's role with the MI intertwined with the delicate fabric of local alliances and the ever-present threat of insurgency. Inside the operations tent, surrounded by the tools of his trade—radios, encrypted devices and maps marked with annotations of numerous briefings—Lima was a focal point of calm precision. He was about to dial one of his contacts, a voice known only as Zulu who often provided crucial insights from deep within insurgent territories. Lima's voice cut through the static hum of electronic equipment as he reached for the secure line. Outside, the jungle teemed with unseen forms of life.

"Any changes on the ground since last check?" Lima asked.

"There was no KYKL involvement in the Sugnu attack," Zulu said. "Look at the NSCN."

Lima paused, his finger hovering above a map scattered with red pins indicating recent skirmishes. The NSCN (IM) had entered into a ceasefire agreement with the Government of India on 25 July 1997. Breaking this ceasefire would be considered a *massive* breach of trust.

"Why would the NSCN break the ceasefire agreement?" Lima said.

Zulu's response was terse. "*You* need to figure that out."

The line went dead. Lights buzzed overhead. Agent Lima leaned back. The military map in front of him seemed submerged in a web of potential truths and lies. The ceasefire with NSCN had been a cornerstone of relative peace; its violation would not only escalate conflicts but could also unravel the threads of negotiations painstakingly built over years. Lima was in two minds about the intel. But the game of shadows was about to pull Lima further into its murky depths.

A few days later, Lima moved to the confines of a safehouse

in Imphal. The musky scent of old wood and damp earth filled the air. Agent Lima sat across from his source, a high-ranking member of the NSCN. Lima's source, a woman known for her strategic acumen within the NSCN, had always been a reliable conduit of information. She was chatting with her eyes confidently locked with Lima's. But her eyes shifted when her phone buzzed. She excused herself and stepped away to answer the call. Lima listened, gauging the undertone of secrecy in her hushed tones.

When she returned, her expression was a carefully neutral mask, but her eyes flickered with an underlying concern. Lima had faintly overheard the nature of the call—a directive to *someone* to return from Senapati, a district nestled in the northern part of Manipur. It was a region marked by rugged terrains, predominantly inhabited by the Naga tribes. Lima's brow furrowed in puzzlement. Senapati was KYKL's territory and a risky theatre for someone with NSCN affiliations. Lima questioned his source about NSCN's role in the Sugnu attack.

"Were you in on it?" Lima said.

She steeled herself. "No."

The conversation lingered a little longer, winding down. After she left, Lima sat in the dimming light with the pieces of the puzzle that were nagging at him. Then it clicked. Zulu was trying to get her cadres to move away from Senapati district. What were they doing in Senapati anyway? Lima reached for his secure line, dialling his superior—Colonel Sobhraj. The crack of his superior's voice felt like the calm before a storm.

"Sir," Lima said. "NSCN cadres were in Senapati. It's a red flag."

Colonel Sobhraj responded with a decisive tone. "Assam Rifles will cordon the exit points."

Lima ended the call, his gaze lost. He was walking a tightrope.

The undulating terrain of Manipur turned into a makeshift

checkpoint emerged the watchful eyes of the Assam Rifles. The checkpoint, a strategic imposition along the main artery from Senapati, bristled with activity as dusk crept over the horizon. Soldiers adjusted their gear. Their expressions were a blend of vigilance and the fatigue of long hours. Barricades were set. Portable floodlights lit up the road. As vehicles approached, they were guided into a single file by the rhythmic waving of a soldier's illuminated baton. Each car, truck and motorbike was subjected to a thorough inspection. The interiors of the vehicles were probed by the beams of a flashlight. Occupants were questioned with polite yet firm insistence.

A dusty jeep, its paint faded and windows caked with the grime of many roads, rattled towards the checkpoint. The driver, a young man with a sharp jawline and eyes that darted too quickly from soldier to soldier, rolled to a stop. His older companion clutched a bag tightly to his chest. The Indian soldiers approached the vehicle, their boots crunching on the gravel. A subedaar with a bushy moustache that bristled with authority, leaned down to peer into the vehicle.

"Step out," he said.

Compliance was hesitant but swift. The young driver's hands trembled slightly before he produced their identification cards. The duo was patted down for weapons. Another soldier, his eyes hidden behind the reflective sheen of his goggles, rifled through the contents of the vehicle. Every compartment, every pocket of space was checked; under the seats, the glove compartment, beneath the faded mats that lined the floor.

The older passenger spoke, his voice a hoarse whisper, "We are just returning home from a visit to a relative."

"Who is your relative? What is your purpose in Senapati?" the soldier asked.

Each answer was met with a nod, noted down and yet the

Subedar's suspicion deepened with the vagueness of their replies.

The interrogation was interrupted as a soldier searching the gypsy called out, "Saab, you might want to see this."

He held up a small, crudely wrapped package hidden beneath the spare tyre: a pouch containing bullets. The two men froze and were then escorted to a waiting military vehicle. They had been caught in the web laid by Agent Lima. The checkpoint resumed its operation. Each member of the Assam Rifles was acutely aware of the night's dark embrace tightening around them. The mystery of their journey and the contents of the concealed package hung between them like a strong accusation. And only a strong interrogation would reveal more.

***

The interrogation room was illuminated only by the harsh glare of a bulb hanging precariously above the table where the two detained men were sitting. Lines of fatigue and fear marked their faces. Distant sounds of the night settled over the camp. Across from the men, an interrogator, a seasoned officer with years of field experience, leaned forward. His features were obscured in the half-light, making him seem more a part of the darkness than apart from it. His voice was low, a controlled calm that held the gravity of the situation.

"You're far from home, gentlemen," the interrogator said. "And in quite a bit of trouble. Why don't you start by telling me exactly what your business was in Senapati?"

The younger of the two men shifted uncomfortably in his chair. He glanced at his older companion, seeking some reassurance or a sign to keep silent. The older man's gaze was fixed on the table. His jaw clenched like a silent fortress.

The interrogator's approach was methodical. Each question

was designed to unravel the lies. The interrogator wanted to know which Company of the NSCN were the duo working for. Much like the organisation and ranks of the Indian Army, the militant groups had their own structure which was rigorously followed. As the early hours of the morning approached, the younger suspect's resistance began to crack. The interrogator knew that one question would break down the maze of their lies. He asked it clearly.

"Which company of NSCN do you work for?"

"We are from Company 30 of the NSCN," the suspect replied.

"Was NSCN involved in the Sungnu attack?"

"Y-y-yes."

"Why did NSCN break the ceasefire?"

"The KYKL's influence was growing in the region."

"Did your leader, Isak Chishi Swu, know of this plan?"

"No." The suspects nodded negatively. "Our brigade commander took the decision to attack the camp."

The detained men, now stripped of their bravado, divulged details that reshaped the strategic landscape: the identity of a brigade commander within NSCN. His name was Agung Sumi and he was the orchestrator of the violence against the camp in which four soldiers were killed.

"Where is he based?" the interrogator asked.

"Dimapur."

The interrogator paused, letting the scenario sink in. NSCN had attacked the Army in a KYKYL stronghold so that the Army would pin the blame on the KYKL and go hard after them. To some extent, the NSCN had succeeded in its goal. But the revelation was significant; the NSCN was in a ceasefire with the government and their cadres were not to be detained or interrogated without explicit permission from the central government—a protocol at odds with the current proceedings.

The detention of NSCN cadres could have sparked a political firestorm, possibly destabilising the fragile peace. Yet, the confession tied these men directly to an attack on an Indian Army camp—a grave act of violence that needed retaliation. The interrogator made a decision. This questioning would remain unofficial, undocumented, a ghost operation that would leave no trail but provide crucial intelligence. Now, the Agency had to draw a plan to deal with Agung Sumi, the brigade commander who had planned the attack.

Agent Lima, along with a select team of operatives, was dispatched to investigate Agung Sumi in Dimapur, Nagaland. The mountain-ringed location pulsed with both the tranquillity of the old world and the simmering tensions of clandestine warfare. Lima set up a safehouse on the outskirts, blending into the backdrop of daily commotion and the quiet despair that often hung over the region. His days were spent behind the tinted windows of unmarked vehicles and beneath the brims of local hats, eyes always watching. Always waiting. The nights were long, poring over intercepted communications and agent reports, piecing together the patterns of the commander's movements.

The markets and winding streets became his field of operation. Agent Lima, dressed in local attire, manoeuvred through the crowds with an air of casual indifference. His keen eyes caught every exchange that seemed out of place. The team's presence in the city lingered like a ghost—felt but unseen. Every piece of intelligence was a thread, and each thread pulled them closer to understanding the network and reach of the NSCN's operations. After days of work, Agent Lima zeroed in on the brigade commander, Agung Sumi. He then met Colonel Sobhraj for further orders.

"We've pinpointed the orchestrator, sir," Lima said.

"What is the plan?" Colonel Sobhraj asked.

"We are waiting for your order to take him out."

He passed over a file, thick with surveillance photos and intercepted communications. Colonel Sobhraj thumbed through the dossier, his brow furrowing deeper with each page. After a moment of consideration, he reached for the phone, dialling the high command with a practised hand. The conversation that followed was terse. Once the call ended, Sobhraj turned back to Lima, his face set in a grim line.

"Permission denied," he said flatly. "The PMO is wary of escalating tensions. They're firm on maintaining the ceasefire."

Lima's jaw tightened. "But, sir, Sumi's actions could ignite further attacks."

"The government fears a larger loss, Lima. If we break the ceasefire, it's not just about retaliation—it's about all-out conflict. Hundreds of lives hang in the balance," Sobhraj said, his voice reflecting the strain of command.

"We lost our soldiers too, sir."

"The PMO is aware already. The official stance is clear—we are to hold fire. No harm must come to the commander."

As Lima got up to leave, he paused at the door, glancing back at Sobhraj. The army's morale had taken a significant hit. Despite being amongst the largest military forces in the world, they had been struck a blow by the militants who had breached their camp, taking the lives of four soldiers. Yet, their hands were tied by diplomatic constraints.

A silent undercurrent of discontent and anger flowed through the ranks. Colonel Sobhraj was known to be a soldier's soldier. He had embodied honour, courage and commitment throughout his command. His presence inspired respect, setting high standards while equipping his troops with the necessary skills and support to meet them. This blend of rigorous professionalism and genuine empathy made a respected leader in the rank and file.

"If Sumi could be neutralised outside our borders," Colonel

Sobhraj said, his voice low, "we will have the cover of plausible deniability."

Lima's morale was restored. He almost had a smile on his face as he let the gravity of the Colonel's implication sink into his heart. An operation of this nature would need to be discreet, untraceable back to the Indian government to avoid international repercussions and maintain the fragile ceasefire at home.

Agent Lima, driven by a mix of duty and the need for retribution, took it upon himself to orchestrate this off-the-record mission. He began gathering intelligence on Agung Sumi's movements and potential vulnerabilities. Operatives tracked his communications and movements, piecing together a pattern that could lead them to an opportunity outside Indian soil. This unofficial directive wasn't recorded in any official logs or communications; it was an understanding, a nod given in the dark that set the wheels in motion. The network of informants did their job, with each report and sighting of Sumi analysed and cross-referenced.

A few days later, the command centre turned into a hub of low murmurs and the soft clicking of computer keys as Agent Lima poured over the latest intelligence reports. The walls were lined with digital maps and photos displaying intricate details of the Brigade commander, Agung Sumi's movements and habits. Lima's eyes traced the lines of text that outlined Sumi's life history and current engagements.

Born in the rugged terrains of Mon district and initiated into the folds of NSCN at the tender age of fourteen, Sumi had grown into one of the group's most formidable figures by the age of forty-five. His rise was not just through loyalty to the cause but also through his cunning and ruthlessness. These attributes made him revered and feared within the ranks.

One particular detail in the report caught Lima's attention. Sumi, despite his power and notorious reputation as a drug lord in the northeast, maintained a strict personal code: no smoking or alcohol. Yet, his indulgences were laid bare in other vices—his weakness for both weapons and women.

Lima leaned back in his chair, a plan beginning to take shape in his mind. He needed a female who could lure Sumi out of Indian borders. He recollected his training in Israel and a former Mossad operative he had met during that time. The name of this operative was: Sherry Ramsey.

And thus, Lima had met Sherry Ramsey in a bar in Tel Aviv to get her onboard this mission to eliminate Agung Sumi. Her terms were clear. She would land in India after 50 per cent of the advance was paid to her. And Lima had already made this arrangement after speaking with his Colonel Sobhraj.

***

When Sherry Ramsey arrived in Delhi, the city's sprawling chaos didn't faze her; she mixed amongst the masses, boarding a train to Dimapur Station. The train's steady rhythm was a faint echo of her thoughts and a prelude to the mission ahead. At Dimapur, a car sent by Lima was waiting for her. Her journey spanned hours through serpentine roads flanked by dense foliage that shrouded the hillside. The car's headlights carved a path through the dark as Sherry sat in silence.

Upon reaching the safehouse, a haven of secrecy nestled deep in the countryside, they stepped into their temporary base. Maps and documents were already spread across the table in the briefing room. Lima presented the intelligence he had compiled—a meticulous account of Agung Sumi's movements, habits and known associates. Sherry absorbed the information with precision, her eyes scanning the documents, committing every detail to memory. Once briefed, she straightened, her stance firm and her decision clear.

"I operate independently," she said. "No micromanagement."

Lima met her gaze, a mutual understanding passing between them. He nodded once, sharply. "Understood."

Sherry turned back to the maps. Her focus narrowed as she traced routes and marked potential points of interest in the complex dance of espionage that lay ahead. The room settled into a charged silence. As her eyes scanned the array of documents and photographs spread before her, one image caught her attention—a photograph of a young girl, barely nineteen.

"Who is she?" Sherry asked.

"That's Sumi's daughter. She runs a bistro in Dimapur."

Sherry's gaze lingered on the photograph. The corners of her mouth twitched subtly. The gears of strategy turned in her mind as she considered the new angle this information had presented. Lima watched, almost imperceptibly nodding to himself as he saw the plan taking shape in Sherry's eyes. Lima simply understood that she was going to use Sumi's daughter to lure the man into her trap.

Sherry's arrival in Dimapur was marked by a blend into the local scene. She found her way to a quaint bistro run by Toshi, Agung Sumi's daughter. Toshi was a bright-eyed young woman with a welcoming smile that masked the heavy burden of her militant father's legacy. She made it a point to visit Toshi's bistro daily, becoming a familiar and welcome face amidst the clatter of dishes and the rich aromas of Naga spices. On each visit, she left behind generous tips that quickly caught Toshi's attention.

Toshi was intrigued by this generous stranger, and began to engage her in more personal conversations. One afternoon, Sherry once again settled into her favourite corner table. This is when Toshi came up to talk to her.

"You've become my best customer," Toshi said.

"Can't resist your momos," Sherry said. "And besides, it's nice to find such warm company so far from home."

Their conversation drifted from favourite recipes to personal aspirations, knitting them closer in the fabric of newfound friendship. On a sunny Thursday, as they laughed over a shared dessert, Toshi invited Sherry to dinner at her home. "It's time you tried some real home cooking," she said. "My father will be there; he loves to meet my friends."

Sherry accepted with a smile, knowing this was the breakthrough she needed. Agung Sumi's residence stood on the outskirts of Dimapur, a stately home that blended modern architecture with traditional Naga elements. Its walls were adorned with local art, and the house was surrounded by lush, well-kept gardens. Security guards were discreetly placed around the perimeter. Inside, the decor was rich with luxury and tribal heritage, with intricate beadwork and bold Naga patterns. Agung Sumi's home was a fortress, disguised beneath aesthetics and cultural pride.

He welcomed her daughter's new friend warmly but Sherry could see that he was already gazing at her bosom. Agung filled two glasses with Zutho, a traditional Naga rice beer. The brew, lightly effervescent, was known for its smooth, slightly sour taste with a hint of sweetness and was a cherished local favourite.

"Try Zutho, our local brew," Agung said and offered a glass to Sumi. "Where are you from?"

"Lebanon," she said with a straight face.

Though Sherry did not like the taste, she didn't stop praising it and kept asking for more. Over the week, she visited Agung Sumi's house several times where Agung often boasted of his organisation, the NSCN. Agung spoke of his own power and command, talking about the resistance he had led against Indian authorities. One night, Sherry and Agung discussed global politics over dinner.

"I never asked you," Agung said. "Whom do you work for?"

"Hezbollah," she said, without batting an eyelid.

Hezbollah, a Shiite Islamist militant group based in Lebanon, was founded in the early 1980s. It emerged in response to the Israeli invasion of Lebanon, growing into a potent force deeply involved in Lebanese politics and regional conflicts. One of the most notable periods of direct conflict between Israel and Hezbollah was in 2006, a thirty-four-day war triggered by a cross-border raid by Hezbollah. This conflict led to significant casualties and destruction, highlighting the group's capabilities and determination to challenge Israeli military power. The war ended without a clear victor, leaving tensions simmering and the region in a fragile peace.

"The struggle has been long," Sherry explained, gauging Agung's response. "Decades of fighting against Israeli forces."

"It's a complex issue," Agung conceded. "Power, land and identity—all entangled."

"Yes," Sherry said, "which is why we seek allies who can support our cause discreetly." She paused. "During the 2006 conflict, Hezbollah demonstrated significant resilience against Israeli forces." Another pause. "However, the ongoing pressures and threats from Israel have kept them in constant need of strengthening their defences and offensive capabilities."

"By procuring arms? Ammunition?"

"Yes," Sherry said. "Hezbollah's strategic position against Israel hasn't weakened, but to maintain—even escalate—their resistance, they need reliable partners who can supply them with sophisticated weaponry. Their needs for arms are immediate and substantial."

Agung nodded slowly, his mind ticking through the implications of aligning with such a group, weighing the risks against the lucrative opportunities it presented.

"Can I propose that I step into this gap, to arm them?" he said.

Sherry met his gaze squarely, her expression composed yet compelling. "Let me talk to our leadership about that."

Now, it was a matter of letting the idea take root in Agung's ambitious plans. Their conversation laid the groundwork for trust and mutual benefit, setting the stage for Sherry's strategic play. As they spoke, Sherry was careful to weave admiration for Agung's leadership and his group's operations, setting her trap with a mix of flattery and shared goals. Her mention of needing arms outside of India was the final piece, presented as a simple necessity rather than a calculated request. By the time they finished their meal, Sherry had skillfully positioned herself as a potential partner in Agung's endeavours.

After a few days, Agung invited Sherry home on the pretext of discussing the arms deal. In the ambience of his private den, Sherry and Agung sat across from each other. The surface of the table between them glistened with the condensation from their chilled drinks. Sherry leaned forward slightly, her eyes locked on Agung's.

"Your vision for the region is truly impressive," she said.

Agung relaxed, the compliment sinking in, lowering the defences of a man accustomed to suspicion. Sherry's veiled seduction had fired some sparks of intimacy between them. She decided it was time to tighten the knot. She moved closer to Agung, her approach smooth and deliberate.

"You truly are a man of depth, Agung," Sherry murmured in his ears.

She deliberately brushed against him. Agung turned to face her, their eyes meeting in a moment fraught with unspoken possibilities. The distance between them closed. Their breath mingled, as he leaned in, captivated by the allure she masterfully crafted. Piece by piece, she stripped off layers of clothing and led him to bed. Agung, blinded by lust, could never see the real Sherry Ramsey. If he did, he would have frozen with fear. *Beware, the Black Widow*. That night, Agung lasted for less than five minutes and signed his own death warrant.

In the aftermath of their intimate encounter, a noticeable change overtook Agung. The meetings that once buzzed with strategic discussions and the clatter of military plans subtly shifted. Agung's sharp acumen, which had always prioritised strategic over personal interests, began to wane under the influence of his new entanglements. In the quiet of his study, Agung found himself glancing at the clock, anticipating Sherry's visits more than the reports from his lieutenants. His decisions, once calculated and cold, now bore the mark of haste and distraction as he increasingly deferred to his desires over his duty.

Sherry watched this transformation from a calculated leader to a man led by passion, noting each lapse in his judgement. Her presence had become his weakness, and she wielded this new power with precision, guiding Agung towards decisions that served her objectives. Sherry decided to roll the dice once and set up a call between Agung and the Hezbollah leaders.

On that evening, the soft glow of Agung Sumi's desk lamp scattered light on the mahogany surface. An open laptop and documents bore the marks of recent activity. As the line clicked, signalling the readiness of the *supposed* Hezbollah leader on the other end, Agung straightened in his chair. Sherry had disguised her team members as Hezbollah leaders, leading Agung to think that he was dealing with the leadership of the said group.

"Mr Sumi, we are looking to procure assault rifles, RPG-7 rocket launchers, and accompanying munitions," the voice on the speaker announced with deliberate clarity. "We expect these to be of the highest standards."

Agung listened, his fingers tapping lightly against the desk, mentally calculating the logistics of such a request. "I can provide these," he said after a moment. "Each shipment will be discreet, to ensure they reach you without scrutiny."

Sherry observed every nuance of his behaviour, noting the slight tension in his jaw.

"Where do you want the delivery?" Agung asked.

"Myanmar will work," Sherry said. "The arms should arrive via the northern route, avoiding major checkpoints. Our contacts there will handle it from there."

Agung keyed in a few more details into his mind, finalising routes and schedules. "It's settled then. I trust your men will be ready to receive the shipment?"

"They will be," Sherry said. "You've made a wise choice, Agung. Your arms will bolster our fight considerably."

They concluded the call after finalising the commercials. Sherry had woven layers of deception. Agung, now fully committed to the deal, had unknowingly stepped into a trap that would unravel his empire from within. Agung spoke to his contacts in Myanmar and decided to visit the country to arrange for the arms.

***

Moreh border, straddling the edges of Myanmar and India, was a region veiled in mist and enigma. Dense forests carpeted the hillsides and acted as silent sentinels. The terrain presented an ideal route for crossings. Agung Sumi planned to use this route to seal the deal which he had so meticulously planned. As dawn broke, painting the sky with streaks of pink and orange, Agung, accompanied by his four bodyguards began his journey. Seated beside him was Sherry. They travelled in an SUV, the vehicle blending with the occasional local traffic that traversed the remote roads of Nagaland.

Unbeknownst to them, Agent Lima and his elite team were weaving their own path through the terrain, maintaining a strategic distance of 400 metres from Sumi's vehicle. Sherry was wearing a GPS device which was constantly relaying her position to Lima and his team. The operation was tightly coordinated.

Lima's vehicle was equipped with state-of-the-art surveillance gear that buzzed softly in the background.

In the command centre, a team of operators monitored every movement. "Speed consistent at 50 kilometres per hour, heading north towards the border crossing," one technician reported, his eyes fixed on the screen that displayed a blinking dot moving through a virtual map of the region.

Lima kept his eyes on the road, his hands steady on the wheel. As they moved closer to the border, the lush greenery of Moreh enveloped them, a reminder of the thin line they were about to cross—both literally and metaphorically. Agung's SUV was moving fast across the remote stretch of road that cut through the dense forests. The quiet of the jungle was broken only by the low hum of the engine from the vehicle. Suddenly, Sherry pressed her hand against her stomach and leaned forward from the passenger seat. She was feigning discomfort.

"I need to stop for a moment, Agung, I'm not feeling well," she said.

With a frown, Agung nodded and the driver pulled the vehicle onto the side of the narrow road, the gravel crunching under the tyre. As the SUV came to a halt, the silence of the secluded area enveloped them. The tranquillity was deceptive.

Then the air was shattered by the sudden roar of gunfire. From their position, 400 metres back, Lima and his team had closed in rapidly, now taking cover behind the thick trunks of roadside trees. The team was well-armed; carbines in their hands spat bullets with deadly precision. Rapid staccato bursts cut through the air. Agung's bodyguards reacted instantly, reaching for their arms, a mix of Glock pistols and AK-47s, returning fire towards the flashes and noises in the dense foliage. Bullets zipped back and forth, thudding into tree bark and puncturing the metal body of Agung's SUV with a metallic clang. The exchange was fierce and unrelenting.

In the chaos, Lima and his team manoeuvred with lethal efficiency. Two bodyguards fell almost immediately, caught off-guard by the precision of the ambush. The other two returned fire, spraying bullets in a desperate attempt to cover Agung's attempt to restart the vehicle.

Lima took cover behind a thick tree, carefully assessing the scene. Spotting one of Agung's bodyguards peering out from behind the SUV, weapon poised to fire, Lima steadied his breath and lined up his shot. With a practised eye, he squeezed the trigger of his carbine, the rifle's retort sharp in the still air. The bullet flew across the distance with precision, finding its mark between the eyes of the bodyguard. The man dropped instantly, his weapon clattering to the ground. The shot, fired over a considerable distance through the slight haze of gun smoke and the chaos of battle, was nothing short of spectacular. The remaining bodyguard was also swiftly silenced by the trained marksmen of Lima's team.

Agung frantically reached for the driver's seat and searched for the ignition key. It was then that he noticed that Sherry had the keys to the vehicle.

"Let's go," Agung said. "Quickly!"

Sherry didn't budge.

"You'll get us both killed," Agung said. "Give me the keys, bitch!"

Sherry pulled a compact Sig Sauer from her jacket and pressed the barrel against Agung's temple. "Don't move," she hissed.

Beware, the Black Widow. Agung's hand froze on the steering wheel. His breath scrambled in his throat as the cold metal of Sherry's pistol pressed against his temple. The sudden shift from companion to captor left him reeling. Disbelief clouded his eyes. Shock. Betrayal. The sense of defeat was enormous, his mind struggling to reconcile with the woman he had bedded was holding him at gunpoint. Now, with his own weapon lying out of reach and his protectors dispatched, he faced the inevitable consequences of his oversight.

Lima, emerging from the cover, moved towards the vehicle, his weapon trained on the figure inside. He nodded to Sherry to exit the vehicle. Lima and his team fired at least thirty shots which not just shredded every ounce of life from Agung's body but also drilled holes into the metal of the SUV.

Lima signalled his team to quickly scan the area for any further threats before beginning their withdrawal. Sherry got into the vehicle along with Lima and the rest of the team. The scene they left behind was a grim tableau of the encounter; five bodies lay scattered around the bullet-riddled SUV in the quiet forest road.

As Lima's team disappeared back into the foliage, the fading echoes of their escape mingled with the rustling leaves. The forest slowly swallowed the violence of the day. Sherry and Lima exchanged a look mirroring the mission's grim intensity. Lima dropped Sumi to the airport so that she could take the first flight out of the country. Then Lima headed to Delhi to meet with Colonel Sobhraj.

Colonel Sobhraj stood at the command centre, hands clasped behind his back. The faint smile on his face betrayed the immense satisfaction he felt. Agung Sumi's elimination marked a significant victory. His chest swelled with the pride of this success. Lima approached, his face a mixture of relief and concern.

"Sir, how will we handle the fallout from this operation?" Lima asked.

"Back-channel negotiations are already underway," Colonel Sobhraj said. "We have contingencies in place."

"Understood, sir. I'll ensure our teams are ready for any media inquiries and briefings."

"Good job, Agent Lima," Colonel Sobhraj added, his tone softening slightly.

Lima looked back at his senior with respect. He realised that leadership was not just about giving orders. It was about making sure the people under you are taken care of.

"Thank you, sir," Lima said. "I learned from the best."

Colonel Sobhraj chuckled softly. "There's much to do."

Lima saluted and left the room, indicating that he would be ready when called, his mind buzzing with the implications of the mission and the unexpected conversation with Colonel Sobhraj.

Later that afternoon, Colonel Sobhraj stood on the lush, manicured lawn of the gold course with a club in hand. The lawn, with its neatly trimmed grass, was perfect for his practice. With a swing, he sent the golf ball soaring across the yard. The crisp sound of the club striking the ball was satisfying. He watched it land with precision near the hole he had set up.

He took another swing, the ball landing perfectly once again. This solitary game of golf was his way of relaxing from the challenges that had been completed. He knew there would be more missions, more battles to fight. But for now, under the waning afternoon light, he allowed himself this brief respite.

The elimination of Agung Sumi was a significant victory, a milestone in his career. It was a moment to savour, even in solitude. The Dogras had been avenged. As he finished his practice, the sky's vibrant colours began to fade. The Colonel took a deep breath.

"Mission accomplished," he whispered (to no one in particular).

For now, everything around him was calm, and serene.

***

The garden's soft lamplight created a serene ambiance as Mr Zaidi and Lucky Bisht strolled through the neatly trimmed hedges and blooming flowers. The air was cool and carried the faint scent of jasmine, making the setting almost idyllic despite the gravity of their discussion. Mr Zaidi paused near a stone bench, gesturing for Lucky to sit with him.

"Sherry truly lived up to her reputation as the Black Widow," Mr Zaidi said. "She devoured Sumi after mating him."

Lucky chuckled softly. "Indeed."

"So what's next for Lima and Sherry?"

"They've gone separate ways for now," Lucky replied. "But there's always another mission, another threat. They'll be ready when they are needed."

The garden fell into a comfortable silence, the distant chirping of crickets providing a gentle background score. The world of espionage was a shady realm, full of complexities and unseen battles. But it was people like Lima and Sherry who navigated these murky waters to keep the balance.

Mr Zaidi finally stood up, stretching his legs. "Thank you, Lucky, for sharing these stories."

"Anytime, Mr Zaidi. Our stories need to be told, even if in the most unusual of places."

As they walked towards the garden's exit, Mr Zaidi looked up at the sky, the stars shining brightly against the velvet night. With a final nod, Mr Zaidi and Lucky parted ways, each disappearing into the night. Over a period of weeks, they had exchanged unusual stories of bravery, courage, betrayal and deception. These would linger for a long, long time.

Mr Zaidi was walking back to his home, where he planned to have his dinner and call it a night. He was sure that Lucky had many more gems hidden in the treasure chest of stories. They'd be told when the time was ripe; and right.

Epilogue

The eight gripping stories of Agent Lima you've just read are slices of reality—candid, unfiltered, and starkly real. They almost faded into the shadows of oblivion, yet Lucky Singh's bold narration transported me to a world where men like Agent Lima tread a perilous line between life and death. These stories are acts of devotion far beyond the call of duty, navigating terrains where survival is a luxury and betrayal is routine.

Lucky and Lima have always been heroes, yet their valour has seldom been acknowledged. I am proud to have uncovered their tales of courage and to present them to the world as they are. I still remember our long discussions, in cafés secluded from Mumbai's usual frenzy, where we spoke about missions destined to remain unrecorded in history. Stories of operations hidden in jungles, deserts and bustling cities—each interwoven with sacrifice and silence. As citizens of this great nation, we owe it to our heroes to recognize their undaunted prowess.

I've always been drawn to stories from the streets, the underworld, and the dark corners of society. But the stories of Agent Lima revealed a realm beyond my usual scope. Understanding the men and women behind these missions—their loneliness, fears and courage—was challenging. Their victories are celebrated in silence, while their failures become public tragedies.

Lucky often spoke of successes buried in the guarded conversations of top officials, of operations that protected nations but would never be known. I realized that these unsung heroes were as vital to the story as the missions themselves.

Yet, beyond the covert operations, haunting questions lingered. How far should one go in the name of national security? What boundaries do we cross, and what do we leave behind? The human cost of these missions weighed on me: for every victory, a life is altered, a mind scarred, a family torn apart.

From March 1993 to November 2008, Mumbai witnessed some of the world's most devastating terrorist attacks. International diplomats offered verbal sympathy, but few acted against the terror rooted in Afghanistan and Pakistan. Richard Boucher even defended Pakistan when I questioned him in Washington about its involvement in the 2006 serial train blasts. You can read more about this in my book *Dongri to Dubai*.

As a writer and journalist, I grew increasingly frustrated with the world's hypocrisy in response to what was happening to India. I can only imagine what our security forces, the soldiers on our borders, and the protectors of our nation must endure. Mahatma Gandhi once said, "When there is a choice between cowardice and violence, I would advise violence." Yet, he never advocated aggression. We, as a nation, are not driven by bloodshed or revenge.

Since writing *Mumbai Avengers*, I've dreamt that India could establish a system of retribution and payback, with soldiers and intelligence agents who, against all odds, seek justice for the 26/11 terror attack. Films such as Kabir Khan's *Phantom* and Neeraj Pandey's *Baby* depict this aspiration.

Later, I realized that, discreetly, the Indian government had been working on a strategy to counter non-state actors who operate under false identities in distant cities. India has now embraced specialized team concepts. The stories you've just read are of those unknown heroes who risk their lives and homes for the safety of our nation's citizens.

As I pen these final thoughts, I can't help but reflect on the shadowy world I have glimpsed. Writing these stories was a cathartic journey—a way to illuminate the hidden and honour those who dwell within it.

We should all honour them. Beyond political plans and diplomatic victories, we should remember the sacrifices of our armed forces.

This is my tribute to the untold, the unseen and the unheard.

India needs more like Lima and Lucky.

S. HUSSAIN ZAIDI

Acknowledgements

The years through my college degree were, perhaps, the most difficult ones of my life. Looking back, I was a spectacular failure. My initial academic promise had faded under the weight of a few events, tragedies almost. I had turned into an average student with sparse clarity on the future and no money for expensive post-grad courses at foreign universities.

Every day, during those college years, I'd have a fifty-rupee note in my pocket. Travelling to Bandra from the far end of the city, railway tickets, rickshaw rides, lunch (vada-pav, mostly) and the occasional movie at Gaiety-Galaxy would be tough to manage in that limited budget. On most days, I'd be broke even before I could get home.

No, I wasn't living in poverty; not by far. I never had to worry about a roof over my head, or my next meal—but things weren't exactly rosy either. I was studying computer science at college. My grandmother paid for the college fee from her pension, may God bless her soul. But I couldn't practise programming languages because I didn't have a desktop. I didn't have a cell phone either. Nope. Fifty rupees a day, that's all I had.

So once I passed out of college, I decided that I never wanted to be broke again. Jobs were difficult to find, so I began working at a call centre. The quick money gave me a sense of security for a while, and then I distinctly remember lacking a purpose in life. Around the same time, in 2004, Farhan Akhtar's *Lakshya* was released; it remains one of the finest movies ever made. The film made me seriously consider a career in the defence forces.

So, now, I wanted to be an officer in the Indian Army; and live a life of honour. I wanted to redeem myself, in my own eyes, if not anybody else's. Much like Hrithik Roshan's character in the movie, I instinctively filled out the form for the Combined Defence Services exam. To my surprise, I cleared the written papers and stepped one step closer to my dream. And that's when it collapsed.

I could never get past the Services Selection Board interviews despite multiple attempts. Not being able to make it to the Indian Military Academy, Dehradun, marked yet another addition to my ever-growing list of failures. My confidence took a bashing. But years of character building were incoming.

Like Tom Cruise said in *A Few Good Men* (1992), "You don't need to wear a patch on your arm to have honour." However, I have always had a lot of respect for those who wear that patch and protect the country. Writing this book has been a redeeming experience in that sense. I was able to reconnect with the 24-year-old me who wanted to serve his country. For this, the contributions of Lucky Bisht, who has co-authored the book, have been invaluable. He brought these stories to life with his myriad experiences.

S. Hussain Zaidi (sir) asked me to write this book; a sequel to his bestselling *R.A.W. Hitman: The Real Story of Agent Lima*. I was hesitant to walk into his shadows. *R.A.W. Hitman: The Real Story of Agent Lima* had sold 10 thousand copies in three weeks. Videos of Lucky and Hussain sir were racking up views by the millions on YouTube. Naturally, the expectation of the audiences would be sky-high. But with Hussain sir's encouragement, I took the plunge and never looked back.

This reminds me of an afternoon, in December 2018, when I self-invited myself to a lunch at Bandra where Hussain sir was meeting his friend and mentor, and writer extraordinaire—Vikram Chandra. For years, I'd idolised Vikram and wanted to write like him, though deep within I was well aware of my incapability to construct even a single sentence that could hold a candle to his towering light. After years of writing fan mail to Vikram, I finally had a chance to meet him. Also present was a young, prodigious writer—Bilal Siddiqi—whose *Bard of Blood* was being adapted for Netflix.

In the midst of such august company, I sat—with no achievement worth a mention. While I was working on my first book (*Mortuary Tales*) at that time, nothing had been finalised. It was just a document on my laptop (yes, after years of working and earning, I finally had one). But the point is, I had a seat on that table just because I was Hussain sir's guest.

That afternoon, I got my decade old copies of Vikram Chandra's books autographed by him and went back home. And then I resolved to work even harder on my craft to justify my presence on such a table in the future. I hope this book is a step in that direction. Thank you, Hussain sir. For all my talent, I would have probably never gotten published if you didn't open the door for me.

To be published by Simon & Schuster has been a dream come true. Thank you Sayantan Ghosh for editing this book and trusting me. Your positive assessment of the manuscript meant a lot. Hope we can create more magical stories along the way.

Lastly, thank you Tarannum. You've been married to me for 14 years. All of this has been possible because you make things easier for me. And thank you Zara, my daughter of eight years, who often has to put up with a dad who works his pretty busy job during the day, and then writes through the odd hours of the night. I hope that when you grow up, you'll realise that I worked hard for…you.

KASHIF MASHAIKH